RiverRun

Adventures on the Edge of Enlightenment

By Kathryn "Mothra" Streletzky

The Edge of Enlightenment
　　　is not calculus
There's no approaching zero

There's only dancing on the
　　　Edge itself
And throwing it all away

Perspective shifts,
And all that is, Is –
Laser light shining through
The Crack in the Cosmic Egg

Table of Contents

Introduction: Mothra's World

I found magic in the river long before having to face losing my youngest sister. It was the magic of a life I forgot to live, one unfettered by thoughts and social convention.

"You never talk about what you do when we're on the river," one of my kayaking buddies who worked for the federal government once remarked. In the Washington, DC region, the "What do you do?" question followed any introduction.

"This is what I do," I replied. "The other thing is just how I get money." Boating was the only authentic part of my life, and I swilled down the river like a drunk at a bar. "There's nothing all that interesting about selling pens and pencils to the government."

In my twenties, I harbored bright dreams for my business career, but by the time my marriage splintered in the last days of 1989, I stopped looking for solace in the corporate world. I moved from Virginia to Maryland, and into my dream home on the wooded shores of Lake Linganore.

I bought an old beater canoe, and then a bright shiny one. And a year later, I ventured off the lake and into whitewater, and my smiles started getting really big. Something about the water brought me back to myself; I felt happy again.

"You'll be back. I can see it in your eyes." That's what Cindy, an experienced kayaker, told me when I faced the humiliation of dragging my boat off the river and back to the car after swimming three of the first four rapids.

Canoeing brought me so much joy, that I continued on through the winter of 1991. Though I had no natural ability, I developed some skill, and a certain smugness about paddling whitewater in a canoe. When I switched from canoes to kayaks five years into the sport, some of the novices joked that now they might finally get to see me swim, and I realized how much better I had become.

By 1998, I had been kayaking for two years. Now when I upset in a rapid, I could consistently execute an underwater maneuver that would roll the boat upright as if it were just another paddle stroke. The ability to execute a combat roll spring-boarded me into increasingly difficult whitewater, where mistakes were likely to have consequences. A number of really good boaters had died in 1997, making headlines in the kayaking world. Often, whitewater took the lives of the uninformed or ill equipped, not those with expert skills. Then, paddlers in my own circle started drowning.

In the aftermath of those deaths, I experienced seemingly metaphysical events on some of my river trips. Things I didn't even believe in; things I couldn't really understand. But I chose to listen, deciding that *knowing* had nothing to do with belief or faith. I changed my perspective because of my *experience*, which I knew to be true. Either that, or perhaps I was crazy.

In any event, these weird little twists on the river opened me up to a broader perspective, and my adventure quest took an unexpected turn.

RIVERRUN

Part I: Awakening

A Visit in the Land of the Dead – Mexico
The Barranca Grande, January 2000
14 months after Scott's Death

" Y ou will never die on a river, and I will always be there to paddle with you."

This message reverberated in my head. *Never? Makes no sense.* My friend Scott died on the day I was to meet him, and now I sensed him here, hovering over the wrought iron bed, delivering this strange message with bad grammar.

I covered my head with the down comforter, quivering with exhaustion and too confused to sleep. I wasn't dreaming. I didn't believe in ghosts, or even an afterlife. I didn't see anything, but I knew he was there. I didn't hear anything; that sentence just popped into my head. I snuggled into the pillows, wanting to hold onto the loving, blissful feeling, but I was too confused to sleep.

I tossed off the covers, walked to the window, and gazed out at the grounds of the *Finca San Bartelo*. My world had cracked wide open, but the cows grazing outside hardly noticed. Sunshine glinted off the distant snow-capped peak of Mount Orizaba.

My two-week kayaking vacation culminated in this stunning end, right here on the ranch Dave had rented for his fledgling adventure travel business. His Spanish now was good enough for him to masquerade as a local in the town of Xico, high in the hills of Veracruz. He certainly looked a bit like a *campesino* with his ruddy tan and dark hair peeking out under a torn straw hat.

I had flown to Mexico on Christmas Day, fleeing the holiday stress of family. Thanksgiving had been difficult, as we struggled to accept my youngest sister's diagnosis of one of those rare and absolutely terminal diseases. The two-week trip bracketed the start of the new millennium, and I desired to leave behind me both real and potential disasters.

Rather than stocking up on beans and bottled water, in case of a Y2K catastrophe, I headed to a third-world countryside where clocks hardly mattered. *"Ahorita mismo,"* Dave had told me flashing his bright smile, didn't really mean "right now" to those who traveled by burro. Better to translate the commonly heard phrase as "in the near future, maybe later today."

That's why I loved whitewater kayaking. On a river, I would focus entirely in the moment, the eternal now – no past, no future, no appointments or time schedules – just matching my breath with the rhythm of the river as it slid downhill and echoed off the canyon walls. Paddling was a Zen Meditation without the effort of trying to think about nothing. Much of a trip was spent peacefully floating downstream with friends, but we heightened our attention when we heard the thunder of an upcoming rapid. Paddle strokes transformed from languid to precise, working with the river's kinetic energies, to twist our way through the narrow openings among a passel of boulders.

During my two weeks in Mexico, I delighted in glimpsing another culture. As my guides and I hauled our boats to the riverbank in one *pueblo,* we encountered the local butcher trimming a carcass into steaks for the market. Another time, we rounded a bend in a river to discover a large family party, with an *Abuelita* cooking up tortillas over an open fire for her large and extended family. These we stuffed with crawdads, fresh from the river, and a piquant homemade salsa. We discovered that everybody, even the granny – even our *gringo* selves – danced after lunch. Occasionally, we surprised villagers who hiked down a mountain pass to bathe in the river, or wash clothes, or to fish. Their chatter resonated with the ebb and flow of the water, as naturally paced as their lives seemed to be. Time here flowed languidly by the rising and setting of the sun.

Scott's message echoed in my mind as I thought back on this holiday vacation. Two weeks of kayaking ended with a difficult journey down 25 miles of the Barranca Grande. Just a few years later, the Barranca would become a popular run as new access roads and trails were discovered, allowing shorter-mileage day trips. But in January 2000, this "Grand Canyon" had only been infrequently paddled by kayakers, and mostly as an overnight expedition.

My host Dave kayaked the Barranca once, a few years earlier, and told me it was possible to run it in a single day. We just had to start our day early . . . and stay on schedule, something we had not yet mastered in the land of *ahorita mismo.*

9

We planned to leave *temprano*, early in the morning, and arranged for our driver to meet us at nine, but somehow *ahorita mismo* wound up with our getting to the river just before noon. We were three–Dave and myself, well into our middle years, finding our youth on the river, and Collins, a sandy-haired college student that Dave had hired for the season. I must have known the run was too long for me, four miles per hour too difficult to sustain. As the only paying guest, I could have called the whole trip off.

Just one week earlier, we dallied over breakfast and tarried too long at our lunch stop on the Rio Gallinas. We discovered that darkness descended swiftly in the canyon. We paddled into the twilight far too long, and a sudden blast of engulfing blackness left us stranded mid-river where we spent the night cold and hungry on a travertine island, knowing that this would make a good campfire story one day.

So I laid aside my doubts and misgivings because the Barranca had a mysterious and beautiful reputation. Tom McEwan, an old-school whitewater pioneer, discovered this gem more than 20 years earlier. He now ran a cutting edge whitewater kayak school in Maryland, and he had taught me the art of the Eskimo roll, which allowed me to turn my kayak back upright when I flipped in turbulent water. I met Dave through Tom, who was well known for some harrowing first-descent adventures.

I too enjoyed the challenge of hard and unknown rivers, and if I occasionally got bashed, well – that felt better than comfortably numb. It was as if the touch with adversity, sometimes a very physical touch, reminded me I was alive.

My friend Scott expressed a similar exuberance when paddling – accepting a little carnage as payment for bliss. The river had claimed him, though, on Thanksgiving weekend in 1998 – and while some learned caution in Scott's passing, I pursued the edge, as if in tribute. The river was a killer with a pure heart – injury or death was a possibility that gave consequences, a little salsa for the soul.

So we drove past the mountain village to the put-in location for the Barranca. Dave said the traditional farmers ensured their coffee beans would ripen slowly by planting each coffee bush under the sun-shading protection of its own banana tree. Dave had married a *Veracruzana* from a nearby village who enjoyed the mindless pleasures of harvesting the beans by hand, and scoffed at the farms growing for the American markets with their beans ripening harshly under the tropical sun. The first rapid glistened through the trees and bushes in dappled sunlight, singing its siren's song of welcome.

"Do you want to run it, Mothra?" Dave asked me. I looked at that first rapid, a difficult one requiring a series of linked turns and cross-river moves through four drops. I walked the road alongside the river.

"Putting in below would be less risky, and give us a chance to warm up." I scouted further along the right side of the riverbank. Running this rapid would test the boater's ability to move back and forth across the river to get in position for each

11

boulder drop. I stopped my scout at the top of the final drop of the rapid, looked up at my companions, and smiled.

"Let's do it!" I said, as we pulled our kayaks from Dave's Suburban. I donned my helmet, life jacket, and the neoprene sprayskirt that would lock me into the boat like a waterborne seal. Whitewater kayaks look like brightly colored, short fat cigars with full decks and only a small cockpit hole that we slither into upon entry, and fasten into with the rubber skirt.

The kayak was the invention of the Inuit, who used it as a hunting boat to ply frigid Arctic waters. Kayakers used a double-bladed paddle to maneuver the boat, and skilled paddlers can instantly roll an upset boat back into an upright position.

I shimmied into my boat, attached the sprayskirt, and pushed myself from the right bank into the river current and made my way to river left, as defined from the perspective of looking downstream. I executed this cross-river move by turning the bow of my boat to point upstream, angled towards the left shore. The force of the current ferried me into the desired position at which time I allowed the current to push my bow around angled for the chute.

Success! Water splashed up and over the deck as I dropped through the chute and turned my bow again upstream, and watched Collins enter the river. On the river, we try to be aware of the positions of our boating companions.

The second drop required a left-to-right move, so once again I let the river ferry me across before I swept my bow downstream for the second drop heading right on a diagonal.

I deliberately skimmed up against the rock on an angle, executing a boof move for the second drop. Boof! I landed upright and at an angle to put me into the slack water of a shoreline eddy.

Boofs, named for the sound they make on landing, are the preferred method for launching over any chute with a definable drop of several feet or more. Generally, it's safer to land flattish in an eddy, rather than pitching straight downward where hazards may lurk.

The third and fourth drops were both on river right and I decided to take them in succession. With no boof rock on the third drop, I paddled straight into the waves of the drop and got a little bit bobbled by their curl, so when I entered the fourth and final chute, my angle was off. And I was too slow.

I never saw the rock at the bottom of that drop, just underneath the surface of the water, but I sure felt its impact thudding through the boat's hull as I landed. Off balance, I flipped upside down.

The mountain torrent was cold, and my head was underwater and I was short on breath. I desperately sought to right myself with an Eskimo roll, but the river hurled me downstream with a vengeance. Why, oh why hadn't I paid attention to the steepness of the run-out?

I felt as if I were skimming down a waterslide strewn with hard, nasty rocks. Shallow, too shallow, I swung out sideways from under the boat and could not roll.

The kayak careened downstream ahead of my body and I dragged alongside wanting air. Air! Desperately wanting to breathe, I guppied up for a sip of air in what I knew would be a failed roll attempt.

As my head tumbled back underwater, my thoughts flew to Linda, my youngest sister, diagnosed with primary pulmonary hypertension, needing supplemental oxygen to survive. Is this how she now lived – always struggling to breathe, always wanting air? Damn – can't breathe water.

Out of time, out of air, upside down, unable to roll, I humbled myself and reluctantly pulled the spray skirt free from the kayak. Swimming out of the tight cockpit was difficult because the water whooshed downstream on a very steep gradient. The boat filled with water immediately on releasing the skirt, and with the added weight, I had to cast it off my body, wanking my knee in the process. Not an auspicious beginning.

I held onto my boat and paddle and side kicked towards shore and then was aided by Dave and Collins. I limped about on shore, collecting the gear, and questioned my judgment as precious minutes ticked by. It was now past noon, our driver had headed back towards town, and we would have to paddle swiftly to get off the river by nightfall.

I never found a sense of balance after that morning swim. "Where's Dave headed? What's next?" My mind winged out of control with fear and worry, and my body followed, always on edge, never adjusting into an easy rhythm. Dave kept looking back to make sure I was following. And I suspected Collins could see my warped inner gyroscope.

The opening miles of rapids were continuous, requiring both mental concentration and physical maneuvering. Often called boogie water, this type of paddling was fun with the right attitude and skill set, or could be both a mental and physical drain, as it was for me on this day. I found myself flipping upside down repeatedly.

There were lots of jagged rocks lurking just under the surface at unlikely spots in the rapids. *Fuck-you rocks*, I called them, though I knew well the river itself meant no malevolence. "Good job!" Collins yelled out in encouragement with each successful roll, knowing how much the inner game of kayaking could affect the outcome.

Every time I flipped and rolled, a bit more water seeped through the neoprene seals on my boat. My kayak hull sloshed with river water, making it heavy and slow.

"Gotta dump water," I called, banging hard into the river's left bank. Hoisting one end of the boat aloft, I dumped out pounds of excess water. I was thirsty too, from all the stress, and drank copiously from the water bottle. The parched, dry feeling in my throat was a sure sign of too much adrenaline pumping through my system.

I breathed deeply to compose myself and reentered my kayak and the current. Dave assured me that although the gradient was steep here, the rapids wouldn't require the technical, linked moves like the rapid I swam at the put-in. If only I could relax!

The three of us paddled continuously for the next two hours – Dave leading as he was the only one who had paddled the river before, and Collins paddling behind me, in the critically important sweep – or rescue – position. My guides protected me as best they could, and I was trying to keep the adrenaline pumping out in a steady stream rather than a gushing torrent that could burn out my body's reserve of this natural chemical.

"See, the rapids are changing," Dave called out sometime early in mid-afternoon. We started running distinct drops with pools below, rather than a continuous torrent. The rapids were still technical and difficult, but they also had slack water and eddies in which to rest.

"It's going to get easier, Mothra" he encouraged. Well, time may stand still in Mexico for us humans, but the big flood from last year had changed this river's character in a single season. What Dave remembered as relatively easy rock garden rapids now were steep drops ending in 90-degree turns to avoid crashing into the canyon's rock walls. And these technical boulder chutes almost always ended with hidden, upturned fuck-you rocks at the bottom. The character of these rapids demanded a kayaker to balance like a top in rhythm with the motion of the water, and it was this particular skill which had

16

been hardest for me to master, and which abandoned me first under stress.

By late in the afternoon, after flipping on the fuck-you rocks at the bottom of yet another rapid, I had totally unraveled. Dave and Collins persisted with cheers of encouragement for having successfully executed an Eskimo roll amidst my exhaustion. But I hated feeling so out of control and pressured for time. After hitting my head hard upon flipping, I rolled up screaming and unleashed a bound-up fury.

"Goddamn! Fuck – son of a bitch!" The curses hurled out of me with venom. In the midst of my meltdown, a part of me watched my own absurdity. The river didn't care, but I felt good screaming and crying at the unfairness of those rocks being in the midst of every good channel. I got out of my kayak, and just refused to go on, as I saw no possibility of making the takeout by nightfall. I had a rough day and wanted rest.

"Do you think you could just paddle on a little more?" Dave asked gently. "The river really does get easier, Mothie."

"No Dave, I can't. I really, really can't do it," I declared. "Maybe if it were just nice bouncy wave trains or maybe if we just had a few more miles. But the river's too hard and I'm exhausted." I knew I could not muster the mental concentration needed for the remaining eight miles. Dave decided that he would push on solo to the take-out so that his wife would not worry. Collins and I would camp overnight on the sandy riverbank we had just passed upstream. We traded gear.

17

Dave took the headlamp as he would likely paddle out at nightfall, and we remembered how quickly night had descended on the Gallinas. We took Dave's extra clothing and food. We had remembered our uncomfortable overnight on the island last week when we packed up this morning, and were glad we had brought along some extra supplies.

"Good luck, paddle safely. We'll be fine!" We waved heartening thoughts as Dave adjusted his headlamp against his helmet, before tearing off into the downstream current alone.

We had a much more comfortable camp this time. Sand instead of rough travertine. Plenty of light to set up our site and find firewood. A camp stove and hot tortellini for dinner. Not bad at all but I was limping about the campsite from the torque I put on my knee during my initial swim, and we still had a big paddle to do the next day. We watched the lights of the high mountain village twinkle in the distance, and it was apparent just how steeply the Barranca canyon fell.

I let Collins sleep, and I took first watch at fire tending. Interestingly enough, at the time, Collins was a finalist for the very first *Survivor* TV series, the one with Richard Hatch. Well, one survivor skill we discovered was that someone had to tend the fire. Without someone keeping watch, it would either be too warm or too cold for comfortable sleeping. So because we had no sleeping bags or blankets, we took turns.

During my fire watch times, I would look upstream in wonder at the twinkle of the village lights in the mountains high above us, where we had started the day's paddling. How

18

far we descended! We were on our own in the steep Barranca, far from medical or any other help, and the only way out was to paddle on through. As I added branches to fire, and watched the lights and the night sky, I found myself singing songs from my childhood, endlessly long songs like "Cowboy Jack" that my Dad used to sing to me at bedtime. I was oddly comforted.

> *Now your sweetheart waits for you, Jack.*
> *Your sweetheart waits for you.*
> *Out on the lonesome prairie,*
> *Where the skies are always blue.*

Singing those songs put me in a reverie, and I thought about my Dad, and his bedtime stories. Then I thought about another storyteller, Scott Bristow, whom I had never met but considered my friend. We had planned to meet in person for the first time on the very night he died. I was out of town with family for the Thanksgiving holiday, but returning home on Saturday so a group of us who were friendly online could share dinner together.

Scott was very popular on the Internet forums like rec.boats.paddle (rbp) and BoaterTalk, as he was a prolific poster of his many adventures and travels. He was young and aggressive and paddled difficult whitewater. I'll never forget watching the video of his final moments, as Scott cartwheeled violently until he was sucked down into the churning maw at Great Falls on the Potomac River . . . .

Still leaves me with a pit in my stomach. Scott, so young, so handsome and charming. There was another like him; Mark rode the bus to junior high with me each day. I didn't know him

19

well, but had a crush on him. Blonde hair, cute, personable, played the drums. He was sweaty from playing basketball when he climbed into the attic to retrieve his fishing tackle. In a freak accident, he electrocuted himself on a live wire. In the Saturday papers, they announced that that his favorite song would be played at the funeral, Norman Greenbaum's "Spirit in the Sky."

> *Gonna send me up to the Spirit in the Sky*
> *That's where I'm gonna go when I die*
> *When I die, and they lay me to rest*
> *Gonna go to the place that's the best!*

Back in 1971, there was no grief counseling in the schools. Mark just disappeared, and we never spoke of him again. Didn't go to the funeral, but I could sing to him now. I sang all the old songs that I loved.

> *Oh, they cut down the old pine tree*
> *And they hauled it away to the mill*
> *To make a coffin of pine*
> *For that sweetheart of mine*
> *Oh, they cut down the old pine tree*

Maybe one of those songs I sang for my ex, Victor. I did not know it yet, but my ex was dead too. So I sang my sad death songs, and remembered so many others who just disappeared out of my life. I sang my songs that night for all of them, and for me as well.

In the morning, Collins and I warmed with spiced oatmeal, and I limped on down to the riverside deep in contemplation. Worried that I could paddle no better than yesterday, and knowing neither of us had ever paddled the remaining miles of the river, I wanted to share my concerns with Collins, but in a way that wouldn't alarm him.

I knew there was simply no other option than to paddle our way out. We both had to paddle the river together and I didn't want to seem a burden. So I talked with my Dad instead. I talked with him despite the fact that he had died 12 years earlier of ALS, Lou Gehrig's disease. We spent the month before he died together at the seashore, and when we were alone, he told me for the first time the story of the creative writing fellowship he had been offered, but turned down, because I was coming into the world. I was stunned by the story. How could he have loved me so much?

I stayed with him at that beach house for the entire month of June, reading bits of Hemingway to him. I departed with a Monday morning dawn in order to drive back to work in the nation's capital. He awoke as I gathered the last of my things together, and made it to the door in his Halston bathrobe for one last hug good-bye.

"Remember, I am with you always," he told me. The imprint of that morning has stayed with me fresh and clear throughout the years. I continued to go to the memory of his love in times of stress, and so he lives on in my heart, just as he promised. He was with me that morning on the Barranca, as I cleaned up our breakfast pots down by the river.

"Dad, I'm scared," I cradled my head in my arms continuing my silent conversation. "I don't want to take another beating on the river today. Can't you do a Vulcan mind-meld and put EJ in my body?" EJ was a world champion kayaker. I needed some help, and knew Collins was worried too. I could hardly walk. How on earth would I be able to kayak?

I liked talking with Dad just as I liked singing his songs – a part of me could recreate his memory and it always felt like he was really there with me. If you asked me about these talks, I would proclaim, "When you die, you die." And I knew that part of him lived on in me, his first-born daughter. The riverside visit calmed my nerves and strengthened my resolve.

"I know we've got to get off the river today," I told Collins with courage supplied from my riverside contemplation. "I'll do it. But I just hope that I can paddle." He nodded as I gimped my way around camp collecting the last of the gear for our boats. Barely daring to breathe, I winched myself into the cockpit and the frog-like position I would have to maintain to paddle out of the canyon, and – wonder of wonders – my knee didn't hurt!

We went through the first few rapids, and Collins checked in with me to see how I was doing. I told him I felt a bit wobbly but was doing fine. Then the bottom started dropping out. The rapids were getting BIG. Dave told us that the river would change from continuous to what we called pool-drop, allowing for a rest between challenges. But the rapids themselves never got any easier, because the recent flood had ravaged and steepened the drops along the canyon walls.

We developed a rhythm for running the rapids, with Collins leading, and I trusted his moves though he also was

22

running the river for the first time. Unlike yesterday, when I couldn't figure out where Dave was going or what he was doing, today I had the ability to see when Collins changed his boat angle ever so slightly and to know where he was headed with his *charc*, his "charging arc" or the angle of intention.

Sometimes an errant stream of current would affect my own charc, but today my intention held clear and strong. Rather than reacting with hurried paddle strokes when I lost my line through a rapid, I easily saw other alternatives and could execute a successful alternate plan on the fly. Most importantly, I had regained composure, which led to the balance that kept me upright and safe on the wild roller coaster ride down the river.

"Damn – wasn't that *nothing*!" I yelled out ironically as I whooshed my way down a powerful sluice between two boulders. We were continuing to encounter rapids of real consequence – not the calming picture Dave had painted for us.

We rounded every bend in the river with anticipation. Would this be another big, semi-blind boulder toss that would demand precision, balance and composure? My god, I thought, at least I was paddling this stuff upright, without flipping. Collins noticed too. "You go, girl!" he encouraged as I plunged down a turbulent drop right-side up and in control.

Did my improving mood have anything to do with the dappled sunlight coming over the mountain ridge, reflecting back in the currents on the river? Or was it the signs of civilization emerging like the little rope bridge spanning the

Barranca? More good fortune awaited – a grove of tangerine trees on an island provided nourishment on a mid-morning break. We reveled in tangy delight slurping down juicy fruit, washing the stickiness off our hands in the river. Life here was lush and abundant. Though tired from the stress and lack of sleep, the refreshment renewed spirit, mind, and body. I was content to be paddling with a new-found friend whom I trusted, and all was right in my world again, at least for this day.

I goofed on one of the rapids later that morning, and my kayak broached sideways with both ends firmly stuck on two different rocks. I maintained the equilibrium of the two-point pin by high-bracing my kayak paddle on the rocky river bottom, the brace against the river assuring that I would stay upright but I couldn't squirm free from the rocks. Today I felt in flow, and did not panic. Instead, I sensed rather than saw Collins in the eddy below, bridging his way across the rapid to set me free. I was glad for my partner's bounding youth and athleticism; I had never been able to hop out of a precarious perch mid-river, something Collins did with ease.

"I think it's best to send you down backwards," he declared as he pulled one end of my kayak free, spinning my stern around and pointing it downstream. I nodded my agreement because as in driving a car, backwards works as well as forwards in kayaking. I maneuvered deftly with a few reverse strokes until I reached the bottom of the rock garden and turned the kayak around. At the bottom, we relaxed and took a late-morning break in the sunshine. Order had been restored in our small canyon of the world.

"So how did you get the name Mothra?" Collins asked me, referring to my Internet handle. I smiled and turned from watching the *campesinos* working their hillside gardens, a sign of encroaching civilization signaling that we were finally close to the end of our river run.

"Ah, it was a silly thing, Collins," I stretched out into the warmth of the day's sunshine and remembered. "I had fallen asleep, fully clothed . . . ."

"Drinking?"

"No. Just wiped out from the week. Then, I awoke at 3 a.m. to the sounds of a moth fluttering around my ceiling fan trying to get at the light. It was annoying as hell."

"So didn't you turn the light off?"

"If only! No, I grabbed a magazine and climbed on top of a Breuer chair – you know, it's the kind with the cane seats and the S-shaped metal legs?" Collins shrugged but nodded anyway. "So you know, when I went to swat the damn moth, I started losing my balance and jammed my foot back on the chair, breaking through the seat. I wound up getting back surgery two months later. But you know, I went paddling the next day, even though I couldn't stand upright!"

"Mothra, eh?" he chuckled. "What's in a name?"

Paddling what we knew was now the final stretch, Collins swerved suddenly to the right side of the river, caught an eddy behind a boulder and hopped out of his boat. I knew something loomed ahead so I veered sharply to get in the quiet water behind that boulder with him. From that safe vantage point looking downstream, I silently named the boulder-choked rapid "Pinball Machine" and decided on my route.

"I'm walking!" I announced on taking a look.

Collins offered to do the walk first, to make sure of the route, but I really think it was an excuse to come back and get me and carry my boat. He reported that the takeout was just downstream, and that Dave was waiting there for us.

The river was finished. I had stayed in balance. I was very happy about that. And now, the full exhaustion – mental and physical – came upon me. My back went into spasm and I could hardly walk. Dave carried my boat uphill from the river to his Suburban, and I had visionary dreams of relieving the pain with Ultram and Advil.

Later, back at the Dave's hacienda, I swallowed the painkillers and dove under the covers on that wrought iron bed, too exhausted for sleep. Within minutes, a soothing narcotic buzz spread out pleasurably upon my mind and body. I snuggled deep waiting for sleep to take me, when I felt a familiar presence.

"When are you going to believe all this is real?" It was my Dad. I didn't hear his voice; rather the words came into my mind with the sense of his presence. He had come to me unbidden.

With him was Scott, my online kayaking friend from the rec.boats.paddle (rbp) newsgroup, who drowned at Great Falls two years earlier. The one who died before the long-awaited dinner party arranged online.

"We finally get to meet." I didn't say it out loud, of course. I just projected the feelings in my heart.

"You will never die on a river." The sentence I received back sounded odd and ungrammatical. Either this was real or I was crazy.

"You will never die on a river," Scott repeated, "and I will always be there to paddle with you."

There is no reality but what you experience. This time the message seemed from myself to myself. Weeks would pass, however, before I shared this story with another living soul. I buried my head deeper in the pillow.

Scott's visit cracked my cosmic egg.

RIVERRUN

Tribal Magic – Maryland
Great Falls, November 1998
The Month of Scott's Death

Marshall McLuhan predicted that TV would bring the world together, but whitewater has never made it into popular culture. For kayakers, the Internet created our global village. Every Monday, we'd hear the exploits from the previous weekend. By Thursday, we'd have analyzed rainfall patterns and be making plans.

The tribal aspects of kayaking were always the most satisfying to me. Boaters would wave when passing each other on highways, and each community took care of its local streams and rivers – painting gauges at the takeout bridges to show minimum water levels for boating, clearing passages through downed trees on small streams, and maintaining relations with riparian landowners.

We had our own myths and legends that were passed down – that of Jeff Snyder surviving a plunge underneath an ice sheath by sucking air from bubbles until he could work his way out from under, or that Jesse Sharp really believed he could survive plunging over Niagara in 1990.

I paddled my first whitewater in the spring of 1991, and discovered something long forgotten, deep and true within myself. Family movies record the biggest smile ever on an eight-year-old Kathy on the Mississippi River in her Uncle Johnny's canoe. A few years later, at Girl Scout camp, I bubbled over with enthusiasm running down to the rack of shiny aluminum canoes.

"Hold it, Kathy," the counselor redirected me, "the canoes are only for the blue caps. Or the white caps. You can take out one of these rowboats instead." Rowing was fun, but I envied the better swimmers who got to slide in the coves where the lily pads collected. I finally learned how to canoe on the lake at Stone Valley, in a gym class at Penn State. Years later, in my thirties, after my marriage crumbled, I remembered that I had always liked something about canoes.

Jesse Sharp actually did canoe over Niagara, though the press reported it as a kayak. A decked canoe looks like a kayak, long and pointy blue molded plastic with a cockpit and a skirt. But Jesse was kneeling in the C-1 and using a single-bladed paddle on that summer's day when he fulfilled his dream of plunging over Horseshoe Falls. I didn't know the difference then either, but the sounds of the news story on the hotel TV pulled me in.

"28-year-old Jesse Sharp, from Ocoee, Tennessee, rode his kayak to his death at Niagara Falls today. Friends who came with him say he believed he could survive the 180-foot plunge, and reported he raised his paddle in celebration and then dropped over the cataract. We interviewed kayak designer Jim Snyder, who had predicted that someday kayakers would paddle over the falls. He said such boat designs were not yet there."

Though I spun the dial round and round, I could not find any more news. Wow! I was not yet a boater, but my heart leapt at the news – someone had once again attempted the Falls, daring the edge. The thrill of forgotten girlhood memories coursed through my veins – the sound like roaring thunder, and razor-pricks of green and white spray.

I was nine years old again, writing composition after composition about the falls in Miss Kasapyr's 4th grade class. I declared my intention to be the first *girl* to go over Niagara Falls and live. My family vacation awakened the daredevil in me. I fantasized dropping over the falls in a barrel like Annie Edson Taylor, a retired schoolmarm, and the first to survive the plunge way back in 1901. Woman had done it before man had learned to fly!

I memorized the names and stories of all the Niagara daredevils that summer, both those who survived and those who succumbed. I "fell in love" with Roger Woodward, a boy who washed over Niagara and survived. He had been in a boating accident with his sister, who was pulled ashore at the very brink of the falls by two tourists from New Jersey. No less a hero was Jim Honeycutt, the family friend who led the ill-fated outing and drowned.

Returning from my reverie, and still mesmerized by the news story about Jesse, I ventured out from the Hyatt and looked for the outdoor store in Richmond where I knew they sold kayaks. I had never thought about kayaking myself, but my heart skipped a beat whenever I saw bands of boaters near Harpers Ferry in West Virginia. I needed to share my

31

unbounded joy at this attempt with someone who might understand, and latched onto a sales clerk in the boating section.

"I just heard on the news that a kayaker from Tennessee attempted Niagara Falls today! Can you believe it?"

"No way! Really? That's incredible. I mean the record is like, what – 50 feet?" He shook his head as if in disbelief. "Who was it? Corran Addison? I figured he'd quit after that time he broke his back."

"Don't remember his name. Jesse something, I think. From Tennessee. He died though." I added sadly.

"Running waterfalls gets so dangerous – anything over 30 feet is risk of life. I haven't done any big waterfalls myself, but I'm driving down to North Carolina next week to pick up a paddle I had custom made. Maybe somebody there knows him."

"Joe Ezterhaus should write a story about him for *Rolling Stone*." I was a big Ezterhaus fan – he wrote the weird but true stories, like Paul Getty getting his ear cut off, or the P.O.W. in Vietnam who maintained a mellow attitude toward his captors while toking away on a pound of pot.

I had loved Tom Wolfe's "The Pump House Gang" story about surfers, but thought Joe could outdo him with a profile of kayakers. I hadn't yet got the picture that I could be a kayaker too. But Jesse's death and the glory of the kayaking life hooked me in somehow, years before I moved to the lake and bought that first canoe.

What the Internet did for paddlers was to take local information and make it global. In 1990, Jesse's death spread by word of mouth, and by snippets in the media. In 1998, when Doug Gordon died on the inaccessible Tsangpo gorge in Tibet, the news was instantly transmitted from a satellite phone to a select email group and then to the world at large via the rbp newsgroup.

At the time of Scott Bristow's death, we relied on telemetered government gauges to find out if a stream or river had enough water to run. In the old days, word spread by phone calls to someone who lived close to the river. Sometimes, the information came from unusual sources.

"I used to call Lou Matacia a lot to get water levels," Roger Corbett, the late author of the *Virginia Whitewater* guidebook told me. "I figured Lou would have good information because he had a canoe livery. And he was usually pretty accurate, too." Roger was a hydrologist by training, and was a storehouse of information about the early days in the sport.

"But I stopped getting information from Lou after I was with him this time. Someone called asking for the level of the Cacapon River, and Lou told the caller to hold on and he'd check. Do you know he took out a dowsing rod and waved it about, and then told the caller three feet? I never called him again after that!" Roger stuck with the scientific method of monitoring measured rainfall in a watershed.

In the early days of the Internet, the best paddlers in the world hung out on rbp along with us weekend warriors. Before the World Wide Web, there was Usenet, a text-only format in which anyone could participate. So prolific posters like Scott and me got to know and chat with each other and some of the most famous names in the sport. We had a social network long before Facebook or even Google.

I still remember showing up to take a week of classes near Ottawa, Canada, with the reigning world champion, Ken Whiting, who kept looking at his clipboard and then at me and then back to his clipboard.

"Where do I know you from?" he finally asked.

"Have you taken a class with me before? No, you haven't, have you?" He kept shaking his head as if trying to place me.

"Does the name Mothra mean anything to you?" I replied, using my Internet handle. And then he started laughing in recognition. Ken was a *lurker* – someone who read but didn't post. And I felt fifteen minutes' worth of famous.

Cubic Dog, the bard of rbp, wrote about the phenomenon in one of his poems, some lines of which were immortalized on the rbp t-shirts we had made up after Scott died:

> *Life on the newsgroup is a strange gestalt*
> *of folks who are brethren at heart*
> *the long distance trippers,*
> *and rads throwing ends,*
> *and those who ask how to start*

The Internet brought all of us together. We didn't tweet or link in; we spilled out our guts to each other and developed intimacy with friends we had never met. That's how Scott from Atlanta got hooked up with David in Washington, DC, to paddle Great Falls over Thanksgiving weekend. Though I had never met Scott or his paddling companions Julie and Joe, we felt like good buddies online, and so I invited them by email to lodge at my home on in Maryland even though I was going to be away until Saturday.

Because they were making plans together online, a whole party developed around the trip, with dinner reservations at *That's Amore!* so that interested members of rbp could meet each other "in real life." But the dinner party turned out quite differently than expected.

Brrring, Brrring! Brrring, Brrring! I briefly considered ignoring the phone to jump in the steaming whirlpool bath. Although it was a warmish day for November, paddling that afternoon without the protection of neoprene gloves had brought a chill into my bones. So although the swirling waters beckoned, I felt duty bound to answer as I was leading a river trip the next morning. David's first words burned into my memory.

"We lost Scott at Great Falls today."

My stomach dropped. I felt numb – the worst had come true. Someone I knew had died kayaking.

"What?" I wailed, "Oh, my god. No! What happened, David? What the hell happened?" I knew a day like this would come, and somehow I wasn't surprised.

The year before Scott died, 1997, was famous because of the number of expert boaters who died on the river. Famous names like Chuck Kern, Pablo Perez, and Rich Weiss. In 1998, the toll continued and got my first personal grief when Doug Gordon died paddling on Tom McEwan's expedition for a first descent down the inaccessible Tsangpo Gorge in Tibet. Tom had been my kayak teacher, and I posted the updates Sarah wrote after her call with Tom each day to the rbp newsgroup.

Now it seemed that Death was trickling down from the realm of the demi-gods to the mortals in my world who paddled weekly, heroic only in their enthusiasm. Doug and Scott, drowning within six weeks of each other, traumatized me.

David explained that on Friday he had taken the paddlers from Atlanta for a scout and successful run of the three drops comprising the falls along the Potomac River.

"Did Julie paddle the falls too?" I asked, feeling a twinge of envy. Almost everyone I knew had started boating Great Falls that year.

"No, she paddled up Mather Gorge and took photos," David explained. Julie was a skilled open canoeist and professional photographer. On Saturday, they wanted to do it again. This time the outcome was fatal.

Scott had run the first waterfall, Pummel, just as perfectly as he did one day earlier. Julie took pictures on Friday, and Scott made the cover of *American Whitewater* magazine posthumously in May 1999 in tribute to the fallen. But on entering the second drop, named Z-turn, he got pulled too far right by the current, spun around backwards and washed into a small waterfall, known as Charlie's Hole. Few kayakers ran Charlie's deliberately because it was a vertical ledge with a strong and dangerous recirculating hydraulic at the bottom. Kayakers who got sucked under had struggled mightily to get free. David said he neglected to warn Scott fully about the dangers of missing the entrance to the Z-turn, because he really didn't appreciate them himself.

"I always knew Charlie's was bad, but I didn't know how bad until I saw Scott in there." That was it. Scott was dead, and his parents were flying in to National Airport and David wanted to meet their plane. He suggested canceling the dinner party we had planned, a meeting of about a dozen paddlers, most of whom only knew each other through the Internet. David now asked me about getting in touch with everyone to call off the dinner.

"I don't think I can do that, David. I don't know anyone's phone number. Besides, they'll want to know what happened. Everyone will have questions. We'll want to be together." So it was that a community of about a dozen paddlers met, most for the first time, and we relayed the news to each as we gathered in the restaurant parking lot.

One couple brought their two-week-old baby girl, Rowan, who had taken her first canoe trip earlier that day swaddled in a lifejacket. The infant's presence gently reminded us of birth and death being opposite sides of the same coin.

"I want a baby. I thought maybe there was a chance with Scott." Yakmom presented Rowan for Julie to hold, and both wept. We bonded with each other over heaping bowls of spaghetti, touching deeply hearts torn wide asunder with a grief that felt both unfathomable and somehow weird, because most of us had never actually met Scott, or even each other, in person.

On arriving home alone that evening, I discovered that rbp was awash in rumors of a death at Great Falls. I signed on and related the facts as I knew them, and promised that David would log on soon with a first-person account. I ended my post with words that would later be read at Scott's memorial service: "Scott was like a beautiful shooting star that grazed across our rec.boats.paddle universe, burning brightly for a time and then disappearing from view. I am glad to have been graced by his brightness and light, even if it burned way too shortly."

Hundreds of posts followed mine – many were read at Scott's memorial service a few weeks later. It is difficult to explain the feelings we shared, both online and in person, as we slowly came out from under our Internet personalities into heart connections. It was as if the most terrible and most wonderful things were happening all at once. Many long-term friendships were forged in the aftermath of Scott's death, as grief linked us together.

As we reached out online, more and more of us started to meet in person. In the months after Scott died, I found myself responding to an invitation from Dag Grada to paddle in the Dominican Republic. CreekDag had secured his reputation online by his first-person recounting of a friend's near-drowning on a waterfall in West Virginia known as Big Splat. When his friend Nick resurfaced from the Splat with a broken leg, Dag created a splint using airbags from his kayak, duct tape, and tree branches.

I loved practicing my Spanish and had visited the Dominican Republic twice as a tourist. This time, I would be heading not to the beaches, but to the mountains and rivers of the Cordillera Central

RIVERRUN

40

Risking Our Lives Together – Dominican Republic
Rio Blanco, February 1999
Three Months after Scott's Death

I clung to the slippery rock face as best I could, water-logged kayak in one hand, paddle in the other. Lodged on a rock shelf between two outcroppings, I felt the river swelling and surging at my back. Thankful for a solid foothold, I gripped into the crumbling rock face with my fingertips. Somewhat stabilized, I looked around and saw Dag's lanky, lean silhouette getting out of his boat downstream. Meanwhile, a crowd had gathered on the balcony, far above the turbines that pumped out the churning water on which I had upset. It was lunchtime at the power plant, and I was the show.

It was three months after Scott died, and I had recovered enough from shoulder surgery to wield a paddle again. Scott and I both dislocated our shoulders, a common whitewater injury, in the spring of 1998. Scott refused the surgery, and discovered that he could hand paddle his boat using plastic mitts down even expert runs like the Green Narrows. He had just started using a conventional double bladed stick again in the fall, which was also the time that I returned to whitewater.

When I took off for the Dominican Republic in February, I had only paddled half a dozen times since my shoulder surgery and my roll was conditional at best. In January, I had flailed my paddle trying to roll up without success on a high water run at Kitzmiller. My paddling buddy Joe Stumpfel looked bemused

41

when I pulled my sprayskirt and swam into frigid Appalachian waters after landing unexpectedly in a pour-over hole.

"What happened to your roll, Mothra?" Stumpfel's eyes sparkled almost as brightly as his glitter-speckled helmet. We had paddled many new rivers together, and a quick roll in frigid turbulent whitewater was critical for the safety of both the paddler and the group.

"Joe, I don't know; I don't know." I repeated in panic. "I just couldn't get the paddle to the surface. I think I should walk out." Stumpfel's eyes darkened with concern. Kitzmiller at six feet was not a river for swimming.

"Mothra, don't be ridiculous. You can't hike out. There's no road, the banks are full of snow, and we still have miles to paddle. We'll go on down the river."

"I don't know. I should never have come. I know how sticky these ledge holes are." Holes are the backwash formed underneath a vertical drop, with a tendency to stop forward momentum. Champion boaters like Stumpfel used the turbulence to spin cartwheels and do other tricks in competition.

"There's no choice, Mothra. Follow my line, I'll keep you out of trouble." And Stumpfel did just that. Joe Stumpfel paddled C-1, the kind of decked canoe Jesse paddled over Niagara. Although they look like kayakers to the untrained eye, C-boat paddlers have a superior field of vision because they kneel rather than sit inside their cockpits. Stumpfel and I had paddled together for more than a year, doing several personal first descents together, and we both knew each other's paddling style well. Even so, I was blown away by how Stumpfel paddled about half that river backwards, always looking out for me, watching my line, pointing right or left, sometimes quite frantically motioning me towards a safer route as he slid backwards into a munchy hole.

"Just make sure Dag knows about your roll problems." Those were Stumpfel's last words to me before I left to paddle unknown rivers in a third-world country with someone I only knew from the Internet. Whitewater was a strange addiction to be sure. I could no more turn down a paddling adventure than could Scott. Even with an injury, I felt I had to keep paddling aggressively because my friends were moving into more difficult whitewater without me.

Some wondered why I pushed myself, pursuing the edge with reckless abandon, and whispered that I was another accident waiting to happen. Every death brings back every other, but I had learned at a young age to bury my feelings. I never mourned for the boy from junior high who electrocuted himself in the attic. I read about it in the papers, and I missed him so much, but with whom could I share my sorrow?

Dag knew about my shoulder problem, and he suggested several options, one of which would provide low risk bouncy fun. But as he pulled out the topographic maps, and talked about a strange steep canyon with sheer rock walls that he had not yet paddled, I forgot all about the bouncy ride and opted for the adventure.

Although the canyon was only a few miles long, the gradient of 116 feet per mile classified it as a steep creek. *Not the Green Narrows.* I mentally compared the gradient to a run that Scott had loved and that had trashed him on his first descent, when he ran it at a high level. Our limited knowledge of what we could expect on the river raised the ante. The sheer rock wall meant we couldn't walk out if the going got too rough. If we weren't back by nightfall, a mutual friend would climb down into the short, deep section of canyon with ropes and technical gear to help us get out the following day.

The lunchtime crowd that watched me dangling from the rock wall, hanging on to all my gear with the water surging up around me, was surely drawn outside to watch the crazy gringo boaters by Jesus, a power plant worker we met while portaging in our boats and gear. Jesus helped us find the trail to the river, swishing his machete to clear out the encroaching brush.

Jesus liked the river and had hiked and swum the entire length of the canyon when the water levels were very low. *He swam it! How hard could it be?* Jesus further informed us that we were not the first to kayak the canyon. Two men, one of whom had a beard, had run it a few years ago, before the hurricane came through. We smiled, knowing that one of those boaters was Dag's friend. After helping me portage my kayak over a steep rock scrabble, Jesus wished us well.

"Que le vayan bien!" I swished my way through at the tropical greenery and gasped when I caught sight of the river against the sheer cliffs. Two huge concrete turbines were pouring out hundreds of cubic feet of water into the tiny

44

riverbed. Like many hydro plants, water had been diverted through huge tubes upstream down to the plant; the amount of electricity produced could be controlled by the quantity of water gravity fed into the plant, which was operating on this day at full capacity.

The turbine blast flowed perpendicular to the main current, creating a turbulent intersection that we needed to ferry across. We couldn't put in below the blast because of the canyon walls. Dag practiced a few rolls and approached what we called the hairy ferry, with the bow of his kayak pointing directly into the surge from the power plant.

Whew! He got blown about and the bow of his boat lodged in a nook of the wall for a second before freeing up and letting Dag maneuver carefully downstream of the torrent into an eddy on river right.

It took me a lot longer to get my courage up. Spooked by Dag's close encounter with the rock wall, I thought to try a high ferry right in the midst of the most violent current. I nosed in several times, but to no avail. Pushed back, I settled into a lower ferry, angling to clear the rock wall by the time I nosed downstream. The idea worked to a point, and I congratulated myself too soon when I passed the location where Dag had momentarily stuck. A surge lifted the right side of my kayak high and I flipped right into the wall.

Upside down, I set up my roll and nothing happened; the blade angle was wrong. So I inched along the shaft with my

45

right hand to find the blade's orientation, and tried a second roll.

"Oh, hell!" I thought as the water slowed for a second. In a flash, I exited the boat, gear in hand, jumping into a minuscule eddy along a "V" in the rock wall. I looked downstream, and saw Dag's back and his ponytail bobbing as he climbed out of his kayak with a throw rope.

"Should I swim?" The thought of swimming this gnarly water filled me with dread. Relief flooded over me when Dag signaled that he would climb over to get me because I hated climbing even more than swimming, plus I didn't want to release the gear into the current.

I kept my death grip on the wall with my right hand, and my left held the gear, which bobbed up and down with every surge of the water. After a few minutes, Dag scrambled over to me with carabineers and rope. Taking the paddle from me, he clipped a towline to the boat. I could now use my hands to work my way downstream along the cliff. I needed a hand climbing out of a turn, and Dag steadied me as I rounded the corner of the outcropping.

"Climbing scares me, too," Dag related as we got back into our kayaks in the slack water just below the outcropping. Looking up, we watched the crowd at the power plant disperse and we pointed our boats downstream. As I reached forward for my stroke, a streak of pain strafed along my left shoulder, the skin there having been rubbed raw as I bobbed up and down with the gear, clinging like a fly to the rock wall. How much worse would it have been without the padded protection of my fuzzy rubber shirt?

We continued our paddling through technical rapids that required precisely executed maneuvers, the difficulty compounded by the high water. The gorge steepened, and we encountered our first blind rapid, one that required us to scout from a tiny strip of riverbank to find a safe route through the boulders.

"The right side's obstructed; we'll have to run the route on the left." First, we dropped into a slot move between the boulders, then we boofed a four-foot ledge to avoid a nasty pinning rock.

Success! We peeked upstream at our accomplishment and breathed out the adrenaline caused by tight technical paddling through surging high water.

"Dag – we're creeking!" I exclaimed looking upstream, and then down towards our next challenge. Creeking referred to such tight technical paddling down a steep gradient. Dag and I both enjoyed creek boating on low-volume runs where our kayaks could slide over wet rocks to give us the thrill of the gravity plunge. But today, the large volume of water being pumped into the steep-walled canyon created swirls and currents making the technical moves even more heart-pounding.

Although the canyon walls were tall and steep, we found enough riverbank to portage that next rapid, which had a keeper hole similar to the one that took Scott's life. *Scott! Remember his story of paddling the Green the first time? Double the normal flows without a guide and near disaster?* As we got back in our boats, I told Dag how I suspected that before the day was done we would have to run a rapid like this – that the scant riverbank could disappear entirely as the walls of the canyon closed in.

The next rapid was juicy, and I bobbled and flipped upside down. As the bubbles swirled by, I attempted several rolls, gave up trying, and pulled the spray skirt for the second time that day.

"Forget the boat! Swim! Get in an eddy! That one, behind the boulder, left, left!" I heard the urgency in Dag's voice and obeyed. I felt remorse about coming here – my inability to roll put both of us in danger.

"It's not your fault. It was my choice to come here." I confessed softly. "Dag, I won't give up."

We paddled some more. We portaged some more. We decided to walk the hard ones when we could to preserve our courage for what lay ahead. Certainly, this river was tougher than we expected. And me with no roll, and Dag with no backup – well, the adventure was just getting to the bottom intact. The canyon steepened and darkened.

Just ahead roared the rapid I had predicted we'd encounter – a difficult rapid that had to be run, not portaged. From some inner place, I pulled together mental toughness.

"Dag, I can do this. I'll run it first. You can back me up." Dag looked shocked that I would offer to probe the monster

48

rapid, but I was sure. My strong suit in paddling has always been that I could find a line through any rapid on the fly. Where others needed to scout, I could intuit the line from the water itself. I was strong. I was sure. I was brave. I was scared. From where we stood, it was a blind curve to the left leading who knows where. I prepared myself mentally to plunge into the abyss.

"Well, look over there on the right," Dag responded, "see that little spot of calm water. It's not quite an eddy, but I think I can land my boat there. I'll get there and signal you what to do. Maybe if we need to, I could climb out and make it back to the power plant from there." I desperately did not want him to do that. It would be a dangerous climb without ropes or gear.

Dag nailed the tiny eddy, and nimbly exited his boat. He climbed onto a rock, looked downstream, and then motioned back at me. We had to communicate by signals because the roar of the river was too strong here. I tapped my helmet in the universal "okay" sign, showing Dag that I felt strong and was ready to go.

Dag shook his head and signaled back with his arms horizontal, to communicate "stop," and then he pointed to his eddy, and made a visor with his hands telling me to come over there with him and take a look.

"Head left!" Dag shouted when I missed his tiny eddy.

I had a lightning instant to choose, and since I was already on the right side, I slammed hard right to an eddy behind a boulder downstream from Dag.

No way. I could not power back across to the left channel.

"We'll need to boof down the right – Plan B," I suggested peering up from behind the boulder to make eye contact. Dag was still standing on his rock and assessed the situation downstream.

"OK, angle left to avoid that rock wall. It's undercut and dangerous. But edge your boat right to deflect the current from the main channel."

Dag led and I followed, and his strategy was spot on.

We were rewarded by entering into a mystical chasm filled with the mottled reflections of light and dark against the stone walls. The water was calm here but created a tinkling music as it swirled up against the sheer vertical cliffs.

Magical! And it felt so wonderful to look around and appreciate the beauty of the stillness of the water in this hidden refuge. Of course, the river coursed onward and soon had our attention once again.

The next biggie rapid looked like something we could manage – punch two holes and avoid an intrusive, undercut house-sized boulder. But the walk-around was easy, so we did. As it turned out, that rapid was the last of the difficult drops.

Interestingly enough, the power plant must have shut down for the day because the water levels dropped, and we were able to peacefully paddle out through the rest of the gorge. Like other small creeks, difficulty was often volume-dependent.

We risk our lives together. The words came to me, from another part of myself, as if in explanation for what I loved about kayaking. The experience had meaning, something I rarely found in daily life, certainly never at work. Focus on the river had real purpose. Rapport developed among paddling companions like the camaraderie of the fox hole.

I tingled with aliveness in every cell of the body, and was grateful to see our driver, Julio, waiting and watching for us at the river's end.

Sex and Death – Georgia
The Chattooga, December 1998
One Month after Scott's Death

"I swear – nothing happened!" David responded to my raised eyebrow as he and Rebecca ("Lightning") walked up the basement steps early Saturday morning. We had descended on Julie's house for Scott's memorial service, and they had fallen asleep downstairs after sharing cozy foot rubs.

Why did I feel judgmental? At 6'3" and 190, David was athletic and classically handsome, and also a husband and father to two girls. Maybe I was just envious. I slept alone on the living room floor, while everyone else roamed the night in Julie's house getting closer.

After all, I had bought that first canoe when I left my marriage, and found the river to be a most satisfying partner.

After almost two weeks of scouring the Potomac daily for any signs of Scott's body, we had convinced his parents that Scott would be OK with his final resting place being the river. They returned home to Atlanta to plan the memorial, and Julie invited a large group of us to stay at her home in the suburbs nearby. She advised us of her two house rules: no eating unless at the dining room table, and no bathing suits in the hot tub. I don't remember much about what we ate; I remember just about everything about that hot tub.

Sex and Death have been enacted ritually across many cultures. Joseph Campbell tells the story of a tribe in Papua,

53

New Guinea, in which the young men coming of age engage in a sex ritual that ends with one young man and a young woman being crushed by the deliberate collapsing of the structure that surrounds them at the moment of climax. Sex and Death are inextricably entwined in the psyche, he tells Bill Moyers in *The Power of Myth* PBS series. Certainly, Scott's death had assumed a mythic impact on me. He and Doug were the modern equivalent of the winning captain of the Mayan ball court who moved gloriously from the crowning achievement of his life into a ritualized execution.

At a certain level of difficulty, Death becomes a silent partner on many river trips. Carla Garrison wrote a phenomenal piece in *American Whitewater* magazine, "He Kindly Stopped for Carla." I caught the literary reference immediately; Emily Dickenson was my Dad's favorite poet. "Because I could not stop for Death/He kindly stopped for me."

In her story, Carla paddles solo the challenging Russell Fork in Kentucky, and broaches against a boulder below a waterfall. She's stuck on that rock and sinking underwater. Eventually, she chooses to let go, and thinks about how she's going to be written up in the accident reports. A mysterious stranger rescues her, and accompanies her down the rest of the river, kisses her soulfully, and disappears with a promise to meet again one day.

My paddling buddy Joe Stumpfel ran the Russell Fork for the first time when I was recovering from shoulder surgery, and repeated the run the next day solo.

"There's no way anyone can really help you if you get into trouble on that river," Stumpfel told me. "I figured I might as well run it alone." I liked Stumpfel a lot, and had even brought him back a sand dollar I found on a beach we had surfed in our kayaks on my first Mexican paddling trip.

During the months I had been sidelined, Stumpfel had taken quantum leaps forward in his paddling abilities and it was clear to me that I was going to have to find new paddling partners. I found it's harder to be left behind by a paddling partner than a spouse, because the memories are pure and untainted. I was the one who left Victor – but it didn't feel good.

I thought about these things as I tossed about trying to sleep on Julie's living room floor. I had cried more for Scott than I had for any other with the exception of my father. I thought back to the conversations we shared earlier that evening, to how connected I felt with all back in the hot tub.

"Scott's eyes were as big as saucers when we walked into your bedroom, and saw your underwear all over the floor," Julie roared, telling the tale of Thanksgiving weekend.

"Hey, they were all *clean* clothes," I retorted. "Hey, I'm busy with every weekend on the river, and work and all. I'm a fiend for laundry, but I hate folding clothes, and often wind up swiping them onto the floor when it's time for bed."

"Trust me! Scott wasn't even going to sleep in one of the guest rooms after that picture. We slept on the Chinese rug on your living room floor, and Joe slept on the couch." Julie sighed – she and Scott were close, but rarely alone.

"He finally told me that I had him that night. I'll never forget it. He said that he was mine. And then, the very next day, he died. He died."

It wasn't hard to talk about Scott as long as we were in company. Julie and David and Joe and every other soul who grieved for Scott connected with my own heartstrings. We sang the Elton John song "Candle in the Wind" together. We supported David when he shook his head in sorrow, for never having explained, for never having really understood, the dangers of Charlie's Hole. "Even after 104 runs down the falls, I didn't understand the dangers."

My own teacher in the heart's path was Jim Snyder, a boat designer and paddle maker who lived in relative obscurity along a riverbank in a small West Virginia town. Jim was the one who was quoted by the newscaster when Jesse Sharp thought to challenge Niagara. Jim had lost four of his friends to various rivers and wrote eloquently on the subject of life and death when a series of six expert kayakers died the previous year.

> *We should remember that they had friends who cared for and appreciated them. And they enhanced their friend's lives and are missed forever. Appreciating the time we had with them is not the lesson. Appreciating the time we have left is the lesson. These guys lived free and strong. Hey, have no*

regrets. They all taught us a great lesson in their passing, but it will take years to unravel. Their lives – and their deaths – were gifts to us. We shouldn't sully the gifts with selfish laments.

"Always remember what is at stake," was the gift Scott left in his passing, interpreted my guru. Jim said that whenever a friend died on the river, he always left behind a gift to the living.

Watching the video of Scott's final moments, we were awestruck that it was not really difficult to watch. He was slammed about hard by the water of course, as if he were riding a bucking bronco, and in an instant the river swallowed him whole, but we could still see his helmet, and then the boat flew out of Charlie's Hole, empty. Had the hole spat out Scott, he would have been immortalized in the carnage section of some paddling video. But he didn't, and so his immortality was to be remembered by those of us whose lives he touched.

I had ordered a paddle from Jim just weeks before Scott drowned. That's how we became friends, in fact, and he invited me to visit him and paddle together on the Cheat River, which ran behind his house. By the time we got together, the paddle was a work in progress and Scott was dead. As we paddled down the Cheat Canyon, we stopped for a lunchtime break at a place on river right where the mountain gorge had heaved down many stones.

Jim showed me four cairns he had built as memorials to his four friends who had died while kayaking. Cubic Dog joined us on the river that day, and he had written a poem to help me through my grief. I asked Jim to emblazon three lines on the paddle he was crafting for me:

> *I don't think there is such a thing*
> *As a life too short,*
> *Only a life unexplored.*

Maybe it was that paddle that got me paddling so defiantly. Death be not proud – you cannot conquer – Scott lives on through me, my memory.

Sex has power too, in times of grief. It was a magical gathering at Julie's house, and we found we were happy as long as we were not alone. Wilko, the dark-eyed Dutchman, had flown in from the Netherlands immediately after Scott died, and stayed for the memorial. Eric, the fresh-faced Webmaster who started BoaterTalk, drove in from Colorado, and would paddle the Grand Canyon that year with one of Scott's kayaks, which we all autographed that weekend. Neither had ever met Scott in person, but, like me, discovered that they loved him and needed to celebrate his life. Lightning and Dancewater, middle-aged female kayakers like me, showed up at Julie's too, along with Joe and David – Scott's best friends and his paddling companions on that fateful November day.

We all knew about Julie's hot tub and her no bathing suits policy, as Scott had debated with her online on that very subject. We had shared so much in our Internet posts that none of us felt like strangers, though many of us were meeting for the first time. Julie piled us up with robes and towels and ordered us to strip.

"Thank goodness! Who wants to wear a bathing suit?" I announced with bravura as I dropped my robe and slid into the tub.

"Oh, what should I do among all you wanton divorced women?" David retorted, perhaps a bit apprehensively. It felt good to be in that hot tub with these personalities I knew so well; we were all cocooned in a soft, warm, watery womb together. And yes, it was erotic, too.

I looked around at my new friends. Julie had the lights blazing – and it felt natural. Lightning sat to my immediate left in all her dark and sultry pre-breast-reduction glory. David developed a keen interest in foot massage and avidly volunteered to replenish our drinking water.

"Water-Boy!" we nicknamed him as his muscular butt sprang up the stairs to refill the communal pitcher. My eyes circled next to the Renaissance woman, Julie, petite and fair, who twinkled with mischief and delight.

"The neighbors had to tell their young sons that we like to take our baths outdoors." Tucker, Georgia had a redneck reputation; we were far from areas where hanging out naked in hot tubs was normal.

Wilko, with his 6'6" frame looking enormous sitting next to Julie, shook his head.

"You Americans have such a sense of shame about your bodies."

Well, maybe, but my eyes were resting directly on his package in Julie's well-illuminated pool. And Eric, the Colorado boy by way of New Jersey, looked about as relaxed as the Dutchman. Even the reticent Dancewater doffed her duds and splashed around with glee.

We spent hours and hours together in that tub, and Julie regaled us with stories about previous gatherings. As we loosened up and into the sensuality of warm bodies and warm water, we started hearing a bit more about Scott.

"You know, I've never been inside of Scott's house. He's got a roommate, but I've never met him. Also, his two great Danes. . . ." Julie's voice trailed off a bit. "We spent such a special time together over Thanksgiving. We had finally gotten so close. And even then, Joe was sleeping right next to us, nearby on the couch!"

That night, sleeping on the living room floor, I listened as Julie comforted Joe. He came over late, after all the socializing, and cried with Julie, sharing a private grief for their unseen partner in the triad that had always been. Eric and Dancewater chatted in the kitchen. David and Lightning had moved the massage party downstairs, while Wilko moved amongst the groups, seemingly trying to get Lightning interested in sharing her foot-rub talents with him. I felt strange and alone.

We all had spent weeks together, looking for Scott's body. I loved everyone in that house that night, and would have welcomed a culturally sanctioned orgy. Not knowing how to deal with my feelings, I turned inward and felt lost in my own vast wells of loneliness.

Earlier that day, hundreds celebrated Scott's life at an outdoor amphitheater in Atlanta that he had built as his Eagle Scout project. An entire Scout troop that Scott mastered lined the walkways leading to the memorial site, and they bravely saluted as many struggled to hold back nearly visible tears. Standing before me was Amy Johnson, a breast cancer survivor, known to me as River Red.

After an opening song, "Circle of Life," a small group of Scouts carried Scott's pack to one side of the stage and set up his tent. David, Joe, Wilko, and another friend, Ron, then acted as pallbearers carrying in the yellow kayak with which Scott had run Great Falls.

"Who are you?" meaning "What's your Internet handle?" was the opening line on the lips of many at the reception afterwards as we continued to meet other members of the rbp community.

The creator of a popular kayaking video series, Milt "Paddleman" Aiken, awed the entire gathering, paddlers and non-paddlers alike, when he screened a 10-minute tribute showing vignettes of Scott paddling his favorite rivers to Van Halen's "Right Here – Right Now." We begged him to run the clip again and again, and he eventually sold copies as a fundraiser for the nonprofit American Whitewater.

The long weekend ended on Sunday with a memorial paddle for Scott along sections of the Chattooga River, the same river that was used as a backdrop for much of the movie *Deliverance*. Still more Internet personalities showed up, including professional kayaker Clay Wright.

I didn't paddle. It was the first time that I had ever turned down an opportunity to paddle, and it was strange for me to prefer to run shuttle, especially as it would have been a first-time opportunity to paddle with so many people I had finally just met. But I didn't. Inside, I was too scared for a run down Section 4, the *Deliverance* section, and too embarrassed to admit my fears, and paddle the easier Section 3.

Instead, I did much of the driving back to Washington, DC, while David and Lightning took turns sleeping in the back of my Durango. I felt a lot of love for my companions, and let myself drift into reverie on the long drive home. I would throw myself into a paddling frenzy soon enough in the months to come.

LIVING A ZEN KOAN

Living a Zen Koan – Dominican Republic
Upper Yaque, February 1999
Three Months after Scott's Death

Adventure comes in many shapes and guises, and once I recovered from my surgery, I wanted to explore them all. First, I pushed myself into paddling advanced whitewater in remote locations such as Kitzmiller in Western Maryland and the Lower Big Sandy in West Virginia, without a reliable roll. And then, in the Dominican Republic, even after the stress of exploring the Rio Blanco canyon, I found Dag's suggestion of a pleasant, bouncy run down the wave trains of the Rio Yuna uninspiring. Instead, I asked about the possibilities of intermediate difficulty.

Dag then proposed the Rio Bao, which would be running grungy and low, but featured rapids requiring technical moves. Never mind that I had just had shoulder surgery six months ago and only executed a combat roll about 40 percent of the time, never mind that we were paddling alone in a third-world country and had experienced difficulties on the Rio Blanco canyon, I felt the siren call of the river asking for more, more, more.

When I paddled, I felt alive. The single point of focus on a difficult rapid was Zen unto itself, and the natural opiates supplied seemed to last for days – and by Thursday night, I'd be jonesing for my next high. Like any addict, I needed a bigger dose of intensity to keep the feeling. But it was more than just a neurochemical addiction; it was the feeling of merging with an entity bigger and better than me. Call it God, Love, Universe, Life, All that Is, Consciousness or the Eternal Now . . . kayaking got me there.

The river was the lover and the beloved, the keeper of the mystery – and my fellow paddlers and I were the priests and priestesses unlocking the doorways to transcendence. Oh, yes, and there was also the feeling that if I didn't keep moving forward, I would soon be drifting backwards. There was that, too!

Our adventure started before we even reached the river. Seeking to avoid a two-hour drive round the mountain, we heard about a dirt road that would cut straight through. "*Muy malo,*" our driver Julio warned, but I declared it to be adventure time, so let's go! Besides, there were *aquas calientes,* hot springs, which sounded delightful since Dag's place in Jarabacoa only had cold showers.

"*Mira!*" I proclaimed gleefully as Julio turned onto the well-graded dirt. "Look! This road is so much better than some shuttle roads I've taken in West Virginia."

We continued on for 12 miles up and came to a pretty little creek that was too low for kayaking, and though the road was getting worse, we were still making time. I still remember seeing a *campesino* walking along the road, and how shocked he looked to see a car swirling up dust as we braked to ask directions.

"*Vayan con Dios!*" his traditional way of wishing wayfarers well, had an ominous sound as we continued on our journey. Not too much later, we were turning tail as the road indeed became too much of an adventure for a Toyota van with bald tires.

"I don't think we can make it through, you know?" Dag conferred with me. "The hot springs are calling, but I don't think we can make it to the Bao this way."

"Shortcuts make for long delays," I said, quoting a favorite line from *Lord of the Rings*. "I guess we should have taken the long drive after all. Do you have another idea?"

Dag suggested the Rio Yaque, a river that was a definite step harder than the Bao. Knowing the upper section of the Rio Yaque would drop 92 feet per mile over its 9-1/2 mile length, I paused to consider, as this would likely be as difficult a stretch of whitewater as I had ever run. But Dag seemed to love this river and promised that we could walk the most difficult rapid.

As we drove up a mountain road to the put-in, Dag pointed down to the last rapid on the Yaque far below. He had named the huge boulder-strewn rapid Jumble, and told me that seeing a picture of this rapid in a magazine had first piqued his interest in paddling rivers in the Dominican Republic.

Now, I knew – absolutely knew with total certainty – that whenever you could see a rapid from afar it would be extremely difficult. This reminded me of how some of the rapids on the Grand Canyon looked from up on a ridge – and at least the Canyon was wide-open big water, without the boulders to dodge. Why, oh why did I persist in seeking adventures?

When we got to the put-in, it was a beautiful sunny day, and I chose not to wear my fuzzy-rubber paddling jacket, which had provided me with both warmth and resistance to abrasion on the canyon of the Rio Blanco. We carried our gear down to an arroyo and immediately started paddling continuous boogie water similar to the steep gradient that I would encounter on the Barranca Grande in Mexico the following winter. This water was not overly difficult, but strenuous because the action rarely lets up and requires constant maneuvering and river reading.

I had smarted a bit as I wiggled my way into the Prijon Rockit kayak; the cockpit was smaller than most and I had developed black and blues from stuffing my knees under the thigh-hooks. I always used rental kayaks on my overseas trips, and so the custom outfitting to my own shape and size was lacking here.

But it was a beautiful day with sunshine glimmering off the whitewater riffles, and Dag and I paddled smoothly from the arroyo into the isolation of the pristine canyon. The sun warmed my bare arms and shoulders, which like my knees, had some minor bruises from swimming on the Blanco.

Gasping in delight, I wished I had the skill to attempt the experts-only combination of a sharp waterfall called *Pico* cascading into the *Escalera Blanca,* a staircase of whitewater ledges and sticky keeper holes.

"I wish I could! I wish I could!" I sing-sang to myself as we portaged on river right while admiring a sheer wall of white rock glistening with droplets thrown skyward by the torrent. A few years later, Dag would bring the *Twitch* video crew here to film kayak professionals Tao Berman and Sam Drevo beautifully running the combination that we wisely chose to portage.

Our day was going well until sometime in early afternoon when I hit a snag, literally, and my kayaking started to unravel. Entering into a fairly straightforward rapid, Dag pointed left to show me some strainers, tree branches which would let the water flow through but would stop and entangle my kayak, which can have deadly results. I nodded, but miscalculated the amount of oomph needed to direct my boat to the safe water on river right. I wound up a little up close and personal but managed to skirt past the first set of overhanging branches. I bobbled a bit on the second set, which put me off balance and caught my paddle blade on the third group of branches, and over I toppled.

My Eskimo roll which had once been so reliable failed me once again and I bailed out of the cockpit, and had to swim out right in the middle of the next rapid. It was painful getting my black and blue knees out of the boat, and I banged my sore shoulder and took a wallop on my helmet.

Here I was, failing and bailing once more. Where was my roll? Surgery had repaired the rotator cuff, but there was something going on inside my head that prevented me from moving into the full extension needed to flip myself right side up when the water knocked me over.

My mood darkened from my own stupidity at being on this river when my skills were lacking, and as if on cue, the sunshine was now obscured by clouds. Truth was, clouds of a different sort had entered into my paddling, and I put on a brave front, seeking to quell the tumult within.

Luckily, the next rapid had a funny name – Hungry Hippo – that got me smiling. And like a wide-mouthed beast, this rapid would have me for lunch if my boof stroke failed to soar my kayak clear of the turbulent hydraulic at the base of the drop. With a light heart and mind, I executed the stroke cleanly.

In the next rapid, I caught a fast stream of current that I could not control and inadvertently passed Dag. Read and run, especially on a new river, was usually enjoyment for me, but the Upper Yaque in the Dominican Republic was as difficult as the Upper Yough in Maryland – and at the upper limit of my experience-level.

I tightened up again when I found myself leading the way. A big pillow of water with complicated currents cascaded off a boulder on the right, and I ran right up on the pillow without the charc, or the veer of direct intention that could cascade me down in style.

Blam-O! I was upside down looking at the fishes again.

Smack! Bam! I created mental pictures of old Batman and Robin graphics as my shoulders and helmet warded off the rocks.

I rode out the rapid tucked under the boat, and tried twice to roll up at the end of the rapid, gasping for a gulp of air on each failed roll. Mental and physical exhaustion set in, and once more I ignominiously pulled my skirt and swam out of the boat.

"I need a break," I told Dag. Once more, I took a beating getting out as my black and blue knees yelped their way past the thigh-braces. My spirit and body were beaten, and I needed to recompose myself. After some minutes, I slid my bruised legs gingerly back into the cockpit. A chill was setting into my bones, and I thought wistfully about the rubber jacket I could have taken to protect me from the cold and the rock slams. My neoprene paddling shorts stuck on the thigh-hooks, making getting back in the boat as painful as exiting.

Yet, in the midst of my gloom and discomfort, I had a rare moment of delight on discovering a weird little frog that had perched on my paddle. Smiling now, I thought of a Zen Koan – letting go of the rope in order to grab a strawberry and plunging into oblivion.

Back to the river, and the first blasts of cold water careened up and over my chest as we made our way downstream. We were in the final stretch now, and it was late afternoon. In another of the trickier rapids, I wound up half upside-down with my head underwater, and though I managed to right myself by turning my paddle into an outrigger with a low brace stroke, I took yet another hit on my hard head and soft shoulder. This was not a lot of fun.

Finally we were there. Jumble – the frothing mess of whitewater and boulders we had seen from the mountain road high above the river. This rapid formed an enormous horseshoe loop full of boulders with no clear way through. Dag said to just hang left and hang on.

I got spun around backwards very soon after entry and careened down backwards for more than 20 yards until I could find room to spin back around. Maybe I should have just kept going backwards, because I wasn't in any better control pointing downstream.

I banged and tossed, and finally a jet of water threw me left of where I wanted to be for the last few yards of the jumble. I finally made my way back right but then flipped over to the upstream side.

Now I was upside down in my kayak and doing body-boofs – right on my battered right shoulder. And yes, I banged my head again, too.

Still upside down, I turned sideways in the current, and was momentarily pinned on a jagged rock. I gulped a breath of air just as gravity caught hold and spun my boat around in the current and spat me out in the pool below.

Out of breath and too exhausted to roll, I began the painful extrication process from my boat. Dag kindly paddled over and gently offered to take my boat, but I was tired and angry and operating from the limbic brain. All fight and flight, I yelled at Dag, "I've got the fucking boat, but I hurt. I hurt."

The river had beaten me black and blue. I could do nothing but lie on my boat and cry from exhaustion, and the release of pent up sadness and grief, too long held as if nothing could affect me. I finally got up, telling Dag that I had some prescription narcotics to take once we were off the river. We only had two miles left and the gradient was lessening to a much easier pace.

Somehow I pulled it together as best I could. I had to take it slow in the pools between the rapids so as to maintain my strength. The strokes on my right side were fairly weak and only marginally effective. But as we went downstream, I was comfortable following Dag and was reading him as a paddler as well as the water itself.

We had a giggle as Dag got caught unawares by a pour-over hole and backendered into a completely upright and vertical position, where he looked briefly at heaven before tumbling back down into the maw. Yeah, I managed to avoid repeating that one, but a little later on, another backwards flowing hydraulic tripped me up and I flipped.

And somewhere in the reptilian part of my mind, the primitive part that had been taking me down the last few miles of river, the part that was incapable of thinking up a head trip as to why I could not roll, that part that only knew basic survival response, took over my body, and the muscle memory just flowed into motion and I easily rolled my boat up again.

Maybe the cry had something to do with it. And another part of me remembered to smile at little blessings.

Julio, our driver, was waiting for us at the takeout, as always. His dark eyes mirrored concern for by my beaten and

71

bedraggled condition. As I struggled with my gear, he took one end of the kayak to carry it with me.

A group of young boys had been hanging around with Julio, and when I stumbled up the hill, one of them came to my assistance. I was glad for the help.

It took me a long while to struggle up the hill, even relieved of the kayak, and when I made it to the van, I searched for some coins to say *"Gracias."* The boy was not looking for money, he was bragging about how strong he was to carry the kayak – and the youngsters flexed their muscles for each other.

Still, I struggled to find a peso to give as a tip. I gladly would have given much more, but we were only paying Julio the equivalent of $8 a day and it was important not to give too much.

Too exhausted to even change out of wet clothes, I took a couple of Ultram to relieve the pain, and started crying quietly in the van, both in relief and in pain. And maybe even in desperation, in loneliness, in all the negative emotions I continually suppressed.

I noticed the big brown eyes of the boy who had helped me up the hill watching me. Other children had gathered and he was proudly telling them the story of how he carried the boat up the hill. Some of the boys lifted an end of the kayak in appreciation of how heavy a load that really was.

One of those kids, a much younger boy, was at the side of my van gawking at me. He looked much dirtier and poorer than the others.

I think he might have wanted to ask me for some pesos too, or maybe he was just befuddled by the sight of this *norteamericana* crying.

But once again, my little friend who had carried my kayak saw me crying, and with a wisdom and perception far beyond his years, took the hand of the other child and led him away.

RiverRun

Moment of Truth – Pennsylvania
Stoneycreek Rendezvous, April 1999
Five Months after Scott's Death

The lucidity of the dream woke me with a start and a knot in the pit of my stomach. I had always been an active dreamer, with a recall of some dreams even back to early childhood. My mastery of the dream world even included "rewinding" my dreams like a movie and creating an alternate plot line when I didn't like where a dream was going. But I never did that in "big" dreams – the ones that I knew had meaning. The dream that awoke me shortly after arriving back from my adventures with Dag was a "big" one.

This river, like many of my dream rivers, resembled none I had encountered paddling; yet, this dream rang true with its unwelcome revelation. During the dream, I stood at a bend on the shoreline between two waterfalls – one pitching into the river near where I stood, the brink of the other right below me. The upstream waterfall was a kayaker's classic – about 20 feet high. It could have been the perfect first descent for a waterfall virgin if it had dropped into a slow moving pool. Below this dream waterfall, however, raged an experts-only cataract with death potential.

Standing between the drops, I watched in horror as a swimmer wearing a blue kayaker's drysuit flushed over the first drop followed by his boat. The man didn't make any effort to get to shore, and seemed to be unconscious. I had to make a choice. I could plunge into the water to snag him, but without a rope or other rescue gear I was at risk of flushing over the second waterfall along with the victim. Nearly paralyzed with fear, but with a moment to make a real choice, I watched as he swept over the horizon line to certain death.

I awoke to my gut clenching with emotion. I despaired at the truth; I was no hero. Isolated and alone, I felt hopeless. How could I let another die?

It was March of 1999; I had just returned from kayaking with Dag, pushing the edge in my own paddling adventures, seeking transcendence under tropical skies. Now Death, and a rather gloomy self-knowledge, had penetrated even into my whitewater dreams. I sunk into depression, and shrouded myself in a cloak of oblivion.

Despite my mood, I continued kayaking, and had volunteered to lead a club trip to a kayaking festival in the Appalachian Highlands of Pennsylvania. The Stoneycreek Rendezvous debuted that April in 1999, showcasing the wide variety of intermediate to expert creeks and rivers that flowed during the rainy springtime season. Many of the runs were tributaries of each other, and could be run in succession – the Dry Shade and Clear Shade flowed into the Shade Creek, for example, which in turn flowed into the lower section of the Stoneycreek River.

Our group of paddlers met near Frederick, Maryland, to convoy out to the Rendezvous together. It had been raining all week and the river gauges were rising. Stoneycreek's river gauge was at seven feet – double the normal flow and two feet higher than I had ever done it. We discussed options as we doubled up boats on the roof racks for our shuttle cars. I suggested that perhaps we could do a run on the Upper Stoneycreek, which would be a personal first descent for all of us.

"At seven feet, Mothra? Absolutely not!" Cathy Hartland, a well-respected member of the club, stated emphatically, "I've heard *horror stories* from Dave Collins about that river at high water." Cathy, slender and graceful as a willow, both in and out of her boat, and the authority she cited, silenced any opposition. Dave Collins, affably known as the Mayor of Great Falls, was a well-known expert boater. None of us wanted to be on any creek at a level on which he had difficulty.

"Well, how about the Clear Shade creek?" I suggested, silently glad to take the pressure off. Murmurs of assent followed – this would be a new run for most club members. We enjoyed an intermediate-level high water float and then made our way to the festival site to set up our tents and party.

On arriving at the Rendezvous, I ran into Cory and Christian, a couple of young, handsome, and athletic kayakers. We had paddled the Dry Fork together the previous winter, and I clearly remember their big "Wahoos!" on that high-water run. They tumbled endlessly when a monster hydraulic caught them unawares, and finally rolled out smiling. At 15 feet, that river had Grand Canyon-sized waves but only moderate difficulty, and a road ran alongside the river, lessening the danger.

"Hey what did you paddle?" I asked, curious about the creeks I didn't run.

"The Shade," they groaned simultaneously as if the ignominy of paddling one of the easier runs in the watershed was just too much to bear. I smiled, knowing that in a year, they too would pass me by.

A bit later, I ran into Rod, a cautious middle-aged whitewater canoeist. He told me that there were unclaimed empty boats floating out of the Stoneycreek canyon, evidently lost by those not up to paddling the thousands of cubic feet per second churning down the swollen river. The lure of the Rendezvous had attracted many who had never even paddled the Youghiogheny, a popular kayak and rafting river in the region.

"Can you imagine trying the Stoney at these levels without having run the Lower Yough?" Rod asked incredulously as he adjusted his glasses. At that moment, the studly young Cory walked by.

"Hey Cory," I quipped to the handsome young man, "Can you imagine that? People running the Stoney without even running the Lower Yough!" He knew I was referring to a couple of semi-famous attempts he and Christian had made on Great Falls in their first year of kayaking. Fortunately, experienced boaters had stopped them before they hurt themselves. They had successfully run the Lower Yough, and didn't realize that there were many rivers of increasing difficulty that they could run before attempting that expert-level run.

Soon enough, I was hearing rumors of a death on the Upper Stoney. A cameraman from a local TV station had shown up wanting to interview paddlers for the news. He told us that a 50-year old man from Eastern Pennsylvania had died on the river. But we were the ones asking him questions. Did he die on a strainer? Was it a heart attack? Flush Drowning? The cameraman didn't know much except that the man was dead, though nothing had been officially released pending notification of next of kin.

"Goddamn!" I told a friend, "I can't believe we've lost another one. I wonder if it's someone we know from rbp."

Eventually, I learned more, talking with one of the organizers from the Rendezvous. Evidently, the victim had paddled the Lower Stoneycreek the day before, and the locals felt that he was pushing his limits and advised against doing the Upper Canyon, which was steeper and more continuous.

He went ahead anyway, and failed in a roll attempt when he flipped early on in the river trip. His friends were also pushing their limits, and could not help him to shore. They had no idea that he would never make it to shore on his own.

His body was recovered 3-1/2 miles downstream, with a gash on the head and a body temperature of 70 degrees despite the drysuit. The coroner ruled that he had died of hypothermia because there was no water in his lungs. But it was a flush drowning in my book – he just flushed down the river alone.

It was only on the way home from the Rendezvous that my dream from two weeks before collapsed into a direct and unexpected intuitive hit of just who had drowned on the Upper Stoneycreek.

"Ben Stone!" I gasped out loud, as if the name were given to me from the heavens as I drove under the pretty arch bridge that spanned the highway and welcomed me back home to Frederick County.

It was *gnosis*, a direct knowing with absolute certainty and clarity, and the psychic shot of intuition hit me as soon as I saw that arc of orange steel. Just like Scott, Ben was a boater that I had never met but knew well enough from rbp to know he was dead too. This one hit home hard, both because I almost took my group to the Upper Stoney that day, and because Ben had the gusto of Cory and Christian, just not their 20- year-old bodies and athleticism. He was middle aged and vulnerable, just like me. He was also a father of four girls, just like my Dad.

Ben and I had almost paddled together that past winter when he asked to join a near flood-stage run on the Shenandoah Staircase. When he admitted his roll was marginal, I refused to let him join my group, as a high water swim at this level could go on for miles. I don't think he ever quite forgave me, though I did arrange for him to paddle on a more forgiving river that day with some friends of mine.

Ben had the whitewater addiction badly, and wanted to move up quickly and paddle harder rivers. Several months before he drowned, he had accomplished a low-water run of the Cheat Canyon – a milestone, a river he never thought he'd get on, and he blossomed with the pride of running that river, which was much harder than the Staircase.

With the Cheat under his belt, and a bit of bravado, feelings I understood only too well, Ben journeyed to the Stoneycreek Rendezvous expecting to snag several new personal first descents. With rapidly developing skills, but still without a solid roll, Ben drowned in the swollen tumult of the Upper Stoneycreek. He drowned clad in a blue drysuit, and flushed downstream to his death alone – beyond the help of his friends.

I understood. How I understood! At the Cheat Festival the next month, I listened as my friend Tom, the guy Ben was paddling with that day, told me over and over how he just couldn't follow Ben down the river because he really didn't have a solid roll and was having difficulty staying upright himself. Tom was a fit and experienced paddler in his 30s, who relied upon his many hours on many rivers to make up for any lapses in natural athleticism.

"Please believe me," he told me as he wrung his head in his hands. "Had I known that he hadn't made it to shore, I would have gone after him anyway. I would have gone after him anyway."

The precognitive dream gave me a full understanding of Tom's choice. I knew from my own gut-twisting nightmare that

I could not overcome my instincts for self-preservation to save the life of a fellow paddler.

Although we're told over and again in Swiftwater rescue classes that our first responsibility is to ourselves, logic and emotion are often at odds. We want to rescue our buddies, but often we just can't – or won't – accept the personal risk. It's a continuing subject of discussion among thoughtful paddlers.

"I would try just as hard to save someone I didn't know from drowning," my friend Norm, an elegantly expert paddler in his 60s, put in. "I would try just as hard, but I'd take more personal risk with someone I knew."

People die, they always do.

Manifestation at the Gauley Fest – West Virginia
Lower Gauley and New Rivers, September 2000
Eight Months after Scott's Visitation

Good days on the river are all alike; bad days are unique and different. I had many more good days than bad, basking in the glow of sunshine, or with the spark of an early frost, but how can I describe the glory of movement through an eternal now?

Eight months after Scott died, in June of 1999, Wilko put together a boating trip in the French Alps that Julie, Lightning, and I attended along with other rbp friends like Wilko. What can I say? France is beautiful. We paddled with the memory of Scott on rivers of ice-cold glacier melt that were far too short for my taste because most of the whitewater runs are broken up by hydro dams.

My strongest memory is not of any river adventure, but of how the Brits and the Dutch couldn't agree on a campsite, so the Americans wound up staying in a campsite overlooking the Guil River run by a native of the Netherlands, while the Brits chose one alongside the flows of the Durance run by one of their own countrymen.

Coming from a melting pot heritage of English, Irish, French, Dutch, German, Czech, and Italian ancestry, I developed an appreciation of just why European cultures remained distinct. They hardly want to hang out with each other, let alone make babies!

From a river-running perspective, I can only report that we dressed for the frigid water and were warmed by the sunshine, portaged a bunch of dams, and never once paddled or even ate together as one unified group.

Happy river memories are all about the people! And Scott, though not with us in the physical, brought so many of us together for small and more personal adventures. After I returned from Europe, Riverman visited the States from Israel. Borrowing a canoe, he paddled a stretch of the Potomac with me and yakmom.

As we paddled down from Old Angler's Inn to Stubblefield Falls, we discussed a river character often called the Dam Builder. No one knew much about him, but he was often seen naked, piling rocks up in formation near the rapids at Stubblefield. Since we were paddling easy whitewater, we set our adventure goal to meet the Dam Builder.

We spotted him far upstream, and approached gently, as he had been known to flee when people approached. As we got closer, we could see that he was actually wearing either a swimsuit or gym shorts. I called out a greeting.

"Hello. We've come to see you work here."

The Dam Builder looked up with suspicion. He was floating some large stones on a bed a Styrofoam to his building site.

"Hi there. I'm Mothra. We've heard about your work here." I repeated gently. His blue eyes searched mine, and then he softened. He spoke slowly as if searching for words, or maybe just his mouth and tongue.

"I prefer the name Omnipotent Immortals," he told me. "Perhaps you could get the government to redistribute the limestone? Limestone makes up only one percent of the earth's surface; granite makes up the most . . . . "

"Granite and basalt," chimed in Riverman, with a side glance at yakmom and me, "I majored in geology; he's absolutely correct."

"Yes, but the limestone has cooling properties," the Dam Builder continued. "Years ago, when the asteroids hit the limestone, the earth cooled and the dinosaurs died. We need to redistribute the limestone again." I supposed he was on to some scheme to prevent global warming.

"Well, that's an idea. Do you have another name? Omnipotent Immortals is a lot to say."

"You could call me Chaozmos, short for Chaotic Cosmos." He then told us he was providing oxidation for the river, and a refuge for snakes, and planting rescue points on the islands for when the floods came. Work as useful as any, we supposed.

"Chaozmos," yakmom interjected, "Where do you get food from?" She asked the question we all were thinking. *From the river? From garbage cans?* Chaozmos looked at her as if she were crazed.

"From the supermarket, of course!" What a wonderful day on the river. Chaozmos became a special friend. When we brought large groups down, he'd still run and hide, but he always recognized me and waved back from his hiding place behind the rock he'd emblazoned with the message: Yesterday was Judgment Day.

The next month, in September 2000, nine months after Scott's visitation in Mexico and nearly two years since his death, I joined five thousand boaters heading to the Gauley Festival in West Virginia. For six weeks each fall, the Gauley River becomes a worldwide whitewater mecca as water levels are drawn down from the Summersville Lake.

As our group waited for the dam release to reach the Lower Gauley put-in, I greeted friends from North Carolina, Baltimore, and Pittsburgh. We all waited together for the water and then would dance our way down the rapids in intermingling groups of various sizes.

This Saturday promised to be another of those perfectly forgettable river days with the low-angle rays of the warm autumn sunshine reflecting ripples off the currents. Well, I hoped it would be forgettable – a good day with nothing much to report.

The previous September, five months after Ben Stone died and not quite a year for Doug and Scott, I had watched a total stranger drown on Gauley Fest weekend. Chris Malisamura arrived at the Lower put-in alone, because it was his first year of boating and his friends were paddling the Upper section, and joined a group from Pittsburgh. He spun too low and out of control into the eddy above the very first rapid, and swam towards the shore and what seemed like safety.

The truth about the Gauley is that the whole river teems with undercut and eroded boulders, with many rock sieves that will let water pass through, but not a swimmer. I remember my first Gauley run, watching in amazement as the famous Tom McEwan came *swimming* through Koontz Flume, that very same rapid.

"What? You're supposed to be showing me the river and you're swimming?" I joked. Tom floated through the flume merrily as could be, holding onto his kayak. Turns out he was surfing a play hole above the rapid, right near the eddy with the undercut rock strainers. When his sprayskirt blew out unexpectedly, Tom just grabbed the boat, now heavily laden with water, and deliberately swam through the big drop.

"It's sometimes safer to swim a rapid. This is one of those places," he told me. Chris had no way of knowing the dangers. And as I scouted the rapid from river left that year, I didn't know that Chris had already lodged headfirst in a dangerous sieve.

I remember seeing people working with ropes in the eddy, and thinking it funny that someone was teaching a rescue class there. I even pulled into the big eddy where he had swum out of his boat and into a rock sieve, before turning and heading down the flume. I only learned a rescue was underway upon arriving safely at the bottom and hearing a desperate plea.

"Hey, we need help! Do you have any rescue experience?" I flagged down a member of our group, Oci-One Kanubi, an open canoeist (OC-1) and rescue instructor. Kanubi offered his assistance, but all efforts to save Chris failed. We abandoned the dead body an hour later; extrication would have to wait until nightfall, when the dam stopped pumping and water levels receded.

Actually, the rescue effort continued as long as it did just to make us all feel better. Chris had succumbed long before. A gloom settled over me. Although I didn't know him – either in person or through the Internet – he had died beside me as it were, and so he became the fourth paddler with whom I felt connected to die within a calendar year.

These memories from last year flashed in front of me as I stroked to Koontz's Flume this year straight-on, wildwater style.

"Eddy of Death, not going there again," I thought looking to my right, and hesitated just long enough for last season's haunting memory to trip me up and over.

The crowd on the shoreline roared in a cheer as I rolled up lightning fast, right at the lip of the churning chute. What a difference a year made – rolling was once again just another paddle stroke.

It felt good to hear the applause for my exciting recovery, as if it were a deliberate stunt to please the spectators, and the chill from the flip refreshed rather than unnerved me.

Like all good river trips, this one fades in memory. About a dozen of us clambered into Kanubi's Shuttle Monster cargo van as he tied down all the boats with such precision, and I remember some of the paddlers but not all.

I do remember Jim Gross, the bearded dew-ragged motorcycle macho man, swimming through Pure Screaming Hell after his braggadocio just above the rapids.

"Oh, Daddy, Daddy, I'm scairt!" he mocked as our trip leader Dan explained the rapid's complexities to our group. Pure Screaming Hell was the last big rapid on the river, and everyone had been paddling with ease all day long. Jim just liked playing the buffoon.

"And if by some chance, you wind up in the hole, pretend you're a rodeo star!" Dan added as final words of advice. I remembered them well as I got caught and cartwheeled about before busting free.

As I laughed my way into the eddy, who did I see but a waterlogged Jim swimming for the same with his boat and paddle in hand.

We also paddled briefly with a real rodeo star, world freestyle champion Erica Mitchell, who was on the river that day too. Although she didn't know me, we both sported the same silver sparkly Grateful Heads kayak helmet, and chatted briefly. Being part of a small sport is nice that way. We ran a rapid together, and then she paddled away with her friends.

After the river, Pete Rutkowski and I headed out to the Gauley Festival itself – a mélange of beer, and boaters, and booths full of retailers hoping to snag a few boating bucks. Pete was a natural kayaker with his slim, wiry build and fearless love of the water.

Like all kayakers, Pete smiled a lot, and knew Mothra from the Internet well before he ever met me. We drove to West Virginia together, awash in the cold late night air, windows open and the Durango's heat blasting all at once.

At the festival, I kept warm by wearing my boof gear – a psychedelic-colored hooded fleece poncho that hit the knees. Not quite the fashion statement – as it was designed to be a riverside changing robe, but I appreciated its fuzzy warmth as the night turned cold.

Fairly early, we ran into Jason Robertson at the American Whitewater booth. American Whitewater put on Gauley Fest each year as its premier fundraiser to support its efforts to protect the rivers we loved to paddle. Jason was selling raffle tickets with a grand prize of a kayaking trip in Ecuador provided by Small World Adventures.

"How many for a 20, Jason?" I asked reaching into my pocket, happy to see another friend.

At that moment, the bearded stranger in front of me turned around and squabbled, "Don't bother; I've got the winning ticket."

"Uh, whatever. . . ." I was startled by his beady-eyed enthusiasm. I hadn't even thought much about the prize. I was buying the tickets because I supported American Whitewater.

"How strange is that?" I muttered as Jason pulled 10 red raffle tickets off the roll for me.

"Here you go. See you on the river, Mothra." And then I reached out and touched the tickets and knew. Instant *gnosis*. That guy was wrong. I had the winning ticket.

That absolute moment of knowing – just as clear and distinct as when I saw the bridge on the way home from the Stoneycreek Festival and *knew* that it was Ben Stone who had drowned. Only this time, the knowledge was transmitted when I physically touched the ticket.

"Holy shit, Pete. I'm going to Ecuador." Pete looked at me quizzically to see if I was joking. "I mean – I can't explain it, but I'm winning the trip to Ecuador. It's like – as soon as I touched the tickets . . . . . I know I've won the raffle – just hasn't happened yet."

Pretty soon I was greeting all my friends and acquaintances at the festival with the news.

"What do you mean?" Leland asked me when I ran into the longhaired steep creeker at the Pyranha kayaks booth. "I thought they weren't doing the raffle until later."

"They haven't done it yet, but I've won. I'm going to Ecuador!" I replied jauntily. "You know, I was going round and round. Should I go back to Mexico? Or try Chile? But now I know why I just couldn't decide – it's because I'm going to Ecuador." Back in those days, the only vacations I took were to paddle – it wasn't a question of what I'd be doing, just where.

When it got dark, they announced they were going to pull the raffle tickets, and Pete and I made our way to the left side of the stage area. As Chris "The General" Koll started pulling winning tickets for t-shirts and hats, I proclaimed that I didn't need to look at my ticket for the warm-up prizes because I had won the trip to Ecuador. Paddleman was standing to my left and documented everything the following Monday to rec.boats.paddle:

For those who weren't there...

From before the raffle started, she kept saying she was going to win the trip. While they handed out the silly hats, t-shirts and dry bags, she insisted she was going to win the trip.

I couldn't believe it when she actually did it!

There were a lot of people there, too. The odds were against her.

Even more remarkable was that when The General called out the winning number ending in 87, the bearded, beady-eyed stranger who stood in front of me in the raffle ticket line – the dyslexic guy who had number 78 – approached the stage too.

"Wait," called out The General, "Seems we have two people who think they are winners." How weird was that. I looked at my ticket three times. Yes, indeed – the winning ticket belonged to me.

"Pete, can we go back to the campground? I feel like I've just channeled the energy of the entire universe into the picking of my raffle ticket. And I don't even know how or why I did it. I'm exhausted." As exciting as it was to have known the outcome, I now felt depleted.

Later, some would say that it showed the power of positive thinking – but I never agreed. I didn't win the ticket because I *wanted* to win – I didn't even buy the tickets *hoping* to win. But once I touched them, I knew I was *going* to win. Another strange and unexplainable event.

Next day, still tired from channeling all that energy, I asked Pete if he would mind paddling the New River Gorge instead of the adrenaline-pumping Upper Gauley. We'd shared a bit of inexplicable magic that weekend, and now I just wanted to bask in its golden glow.

The day was warm and sunny, and the river was deserted since everyone else was over at the Gauley. We blissfully weaved our way down the Gorge that the oldest river in North American had carved, the oldest river that was called New.

Though we spent a wonderful splashy day floating the river together, I don't have a single memory of running any particular rapid. Maybe Scott was there too, paddling with me as he had that past January in Mexico. It was a good day on the river.

The Music of the Andes – Ecuador
Rio Quijos, November 2000
11 Months after Scott's Visitation

I had flown to Ecuador with high expectations, imagining a magical vacation. Dan Dunlap, author of *World Whitewater* and known to me on rbp as JDD RIO, had emailed me after I crowed about winning the raffle prize at Gauley Fest. Turns out that Dan was going to be there at the same time and we made plans to meet. No formal plans, but the rivers were known and we were boaters and sure to run into each other.

I had never been to South America, and was excited at the prospect of seeing the Andes. Picked up in Quito by Don, my guide, I hardly noticed that we were at 9,000 feet because the mountain peaks along the road to Baeza were so much higher.

"You're really lucky," Don broke out in a broad smile on his tanned and weather lined face as we drove. "It's a rare treat to be able to see all three of our glacier capped volcanoes."

"It's amazing. Who would have thought that there would be *snow* at the *equator?*" I wondered aloud.

"It's the elevation. We're looking at 18 to 20 thousand feet. Many of our rivers are glacier fed." Don had been guiding in Ecuador for quite a few years now.

"Nothing like our gentle Appalachians, that's for sure. Our mountains are venerable, but they don't even collect snow pack. We're like farmers back East – constantly watching for

95

rain." Up ahead I could see a roadblock of some sort, and soldiers with guns. We were asked to show our passports and identification, but unlike Mexico, there was no attempt to hustle us for money.

"Government here is concerned with kidnappings and the Colombians. There's the oil pipeline." Don pointed to the left side of the road where a huge metal pipe, tall as a man, ran on and on as far as the eye could see. "Oil. Even when we get to the rainforest, you'll see development. It's just this year that the government here got rid of their own currency and standardized on the U.S. dollar."

"Hey look, a blue Morpho!" I cried out spotting the electric blue creature much bigger than any butterfly I had seen. We pulled into the riverfront land where Small World Adventures has established its base. Delighted at having *won* a free vacation donated to the raffle, I had booked and paid for a second week of my kayaking vacation.

I discovered that for the first week, I was once again the only client. There would be a group coming in for week two. Not being friends with Don the way I was with Dave made it seem a little lonely – more so since he seemed to have a relationship with Nancy, the other guide, an entomologist with birdlike features. Having no one to hang with, I practiced Spanish with Maria, our cook.

"*Que bueno!*" I told her, and retired early feeling a wave of melancholia. Sadness had become a paddling partner, more and more. I had allayed those feelings by pushing on and on, for a time. But now, often I would drive two hours to a river, get out of my car and say – no, I don't feel like paddling, not today.

The first time that happened was in Atlanta after Scott's Memorial, and then it happened again in the spring after Ben drowned on the Stoney. This past winter, those feelings had gripped me again, harder and more frequently – and beneath it all, laid a silent grief in knowing Linda, my sister, was going to die, and there was nothing I or anyone on earth could do about it.

The next morning, I really didn't feel like paddling but the Quijos rapids beckoned outside of our veranda, and Nancy and Don helped me outfit a kayak of the same style I paddled at home. Nancy led down the river until we came to Gringos Revueltos, with a hole at the bottom ready to scramble anyone missing their line. That would be me.

Over and over I cartwheeled in the froth that spun me. Never once did I consider abandoning my boat, so violent was the window-shading I endured. Instead, I sought to suck in a quick breath when I could and maintained a death grip on my paddle while the hydraulic spun my boat over and over again. After 40 seconds or so, the hole spat me free. Dizzy and disoriented, I rolled up on the third attempt.

"We've never seen a paying guest come out of that hole in their boat," Don told me with a smile. "We do have video of one of our guides in there. We'll show it to you tonight." We paddled over to a nice flat beach with a view of the Revueltos drop.

"OK. Can we call this lunch? I've got to rest." After munching, I lay down in the sun. Almost an hour later, I got up and a whoosh of snot and water came draining out of my sinuses. I guess that's where I picked up the bug that laid me up a few days later.

I got to paddle two more rivers. The first was creeky, and afterwards we stopped at a hot springs with many rock-lined pools of varying temperatures. We made our way into the Ecuadorian rainforest, and the town where JDD RIO and I were likely to meet. There, we paddled a bouncy Rio that was a cross between the New River Gorge and the Dry Fork of the Cheat. In a word – Fun!

"Have you seen Dan Dunlap?" I asked every boater I met in Tena without success. By the time we returned to our hotel decorated with the wood of the sacred ceiba tree, I was too sick to watch the Bush-Gore election night TV coverage.

I tossed and turned in the darkened hotel room, eating Zithromax as if it were Chiclets. I had doubled down on dosage, afraid that the severe respiratory infection would go into pneumonia, so I changed my reservations, and headed back to Maryland.

Telling no one I was home, I slept for a week. When I finally felt well enough to click on the computer, the rbp headline shocked me. Dan had died on his first river run, a tributary of the Upper Toachi, on the very day I arrived.

"No! No! No! No! No!" I screamed to the four walls of my bedroom. The wail of protest came from deep inside of me.

98

I had known something was wrong; Dan Dunlap and I should have met each other and paddled together in Ecuador.

" Fuck November!" I screamed into my pillow. "What's with fucking November?" I felt cursed. Scott died in November. Linda got diagnosed in November. And now Dan died in November.

"Why does everybody fucking die on the day they're supposed to meet me?" I screamed into my pillow. "November – a fucking trifecta of misery."

Dan had missed a critical eddy above a class 6 drop, a risk-of-life waterfall that not even experts would willingly run. He survived the drop, though, and died during the several hours that his friends spent hauling him up the sheer rock face.

Dan's death reminded me of an accident that occurred in the Pacific Northwest a few years earlier. A much younger and more fit boater wound up hospitalized with kidney failure after a harrowing rescue where he was winched up a cliff.

I read the story in *American Whitewater* about how the victim literally foamed at the mouth by the time he got pulled up. Dan, a successful lawyer in his 40s, suffered a heart attack, crucified by the strain and a lack of oxygen.

Different scenario, but very likely how my sister would die. Pulmonary hypertension, just like the stress of getting hauled up a cliff with a rope under the armpits, makes it hard for the heart to pump. She'd likely die in a pool of blood, as a major artery burst. It would put too much strain on the heart and respiration.

I thought of Dan – what could have helped him? Maybe a webbing harness strung through the legs? I wanted no more riverside deaths from hauling. I posted my ideas on various forums, and soon a question came from a reader of Boater Talk asking for specifics of Dan's death.

"Christie," I told her after giving her the facts as I knew them, "something else happened. It was the weirdest thing. As my homebound jet soared over Quito and those spectacular mountains, I started hearing very distinct Andean melodies. Flutes, guitars, percussion – all very clear."

"Really? Dan was quite musical you know. We were Butte Irish, poor but lyrical." Christie and Dan were college sweethearts many years ago in the Montana mining town.

"Well, I assure you, I am *not* musical, and it was the damnedest thing – I heard four or five distinct songs playing for me clear as day in my head. I felt like Mozart or something – the music was just coming to me unbidden and I decided to just enjoy the concert. The music ended when we left the Andes."

A few weeks later, I attended a slide show by Tom McEwan about the fateful expedition in Tibet where Doug Gordon drowned on the Tsangpo. After the presentation, I bought a copy of *Courting the Diamond Sow*, Wick Walker's memoir of the expedition. This book quoted journal entries by Jamie McEwan, Tom's brother and the whitewater bronze medalist from the 1972 Olympics, who was also Doug's best friend.

100

THE MUSIC OF THE ANDES

After Doug was sucked under the swollen river, never to be seen again, Jamie and the other boaters scoured the riverbanks looking for any sign of Doug's body. As Jamie retraced his steps back to the accident site, he passed a bend in the river that created a swirling eddy, and he could swear that he heard Doug call, "Jamie!" But there was no one.

Afterwards, he swore he heard voices in the water, and the sounds of children and laughter. Voices that called him back to life, as the Music of the Andes sang to me. I remembered, too the gathering outside the restaurant the night Scott drowned, and how the starlight reflected in baby Rowan's eyes comforted Julie as she held the infant and rocked her on that November evening just two years ago.

My perceptions of birth and death were changing. I no longer spoke of life and death, because it seemed that life had no opposite, and that birth and death were inextricably joined in a great transcendent force.

Scott visited me in Mexico last winter, with my Dad, who continued speaking with me in dreams. Could Dan be reaching out too, through the Music of the Andes, communicating through a chink in the cosmic egg with those timeless, haunting melodies?

In less than a year, my perspectives on the survival of consciousness had shifted entirely. Death now signified transition – like drops of water evaporating from a river and becoming clouds.

Intimations of Mortality – West Virginia
Tygart River, July 2001
18 Months after Scott's Visitation

By 2001, I found it harder and harder to find joy on the river. Garland Reece, a fellow club member, drowned March that year, stuffed against a log pile on a high water run of the James in Richmond, Virginia. Like my sister Linda, Garland struggled with an incurable illness, so he grabbed the chance to paddle on days when he felt well.

"He told me he wanted to die with his boots on, like Dale Earnhardt," his sister told me at the funeral, which followed closely on the heels of the NASCAR driver's death crash. The funeral procession had long lines of kayak-topped cars, and we sang "May the Circle be Unbroken" at his gravesite.

In his memory, I trained and taught Swiftwater rescue classes with a local paddling club; we even demonstrated how to make a harness with webbing and carabineers in case anyone ever needed to be hauled up a cliff.

That July weekend, though, I paddled just for fun, with friends, as in the old days. We had paddled the Cheat on Saturday, and the only accident we had was around the fire pit at Teter's Campground in Preston County, West Virginia.

"We grew up being told the river was dangerous," our host explained around the campfire, "so I've never been on it." Ralph grew up locally in this Appalachian highland, where many swift-flowing creeks feed into the mighty Cheat Canyon.

103

"And after Vietnam, I sure didn't want to go in any rivers," Ralph looked up, and then away while he ruffled his parrot Tarzan's feathers. "That was my mission, to wade in the river and wait for the Viet Cong. Even after they awarded me a Purple Heart, I was sent back in that damn river. That's not right; I kept getting sent back to die. It doesn't get better with time; it gets worse."

Ralph suffered from post-traumatic stress disorder and was disabled from his job with the railroad. Running a riverside campground was his second career and a finer campground host no paddler will ever find. Ralph was in a talkative mood that evening, and stoked the campfire.

Ralph bought Tarzan when he acquired the campground and in just a few years the bird had amassed a vocabulary of hundreds of words. The gregarious nature of running a campground must have stimulated his development. Tarzan only whistled at girls, and would exclaim what seemed to be appropriate phrases in the moment. We never really knew how much that bird understood, but no one doubted his love for Ralph.

So it happened that we were sitting around the campfire, planning our trip to the Arden section of the Tygart for the morrow, when Dick decided to take Tarzan from Ralph and bring him over to our side of the fire.

Did I mention that Tarzan loved Ralph? Well, the dang bird got separation anxiety and forgot his wings were clipped and flew to Ralph in the most direct way possible. Or at least tried to fly to Ralph – his wings failed and he dropped right into the fire and its burning coals.

I screamed. And next to me, cool as a cucumber, sprang Pete Rutkowski, my friend from Gauley Fest weekend, into action. Pete reached deftly into the fire, picked up the bird and returned him to Ralph before the screech died in my throat. Of such action are heroes made.

Five of us set out that Sunday morning for the Tygart. One was Ed Evangelidi, who looked a bit like a laughing Buddha, wearing a frayed life-jacket two sizes too small, and an open canoe as long as it was tattered. Everyone knew ED, as the back of his sun-bleached orange life jacket proclaimed in capital letters; he was unmistakable even at a distance, paddling that canoe with an extra-long double bladed kayak paddle. Wes Mills – an all- around solid guy and paddler who rarely made mistakes on the river, only in his choice of women – seemed like he was always getting divorced and remarried. Dick Pierce, a professor of law who started kayaking in his 50s, who had swum unscathed out of more predicaments on the river than anyone I knew except maybe myself. And Pete Rutkowski, whom I had always liked, even before I met him. Pete shared the same last name as, but was no relation of, a childhood friend of mine with an older brother who had hung himself with a belt as he entered adolescence.

The Arden section of the Tygart is in a remote section of West Virginia that is almost otherworldly. The first time I ever visited Arden, I declared, should I ever need to hide out from the law, I would come here for backwoods isolation. It was

105

even more isolated than the section of northeastern Pennsylvania where Patty Hearst and the SLA hid for months from the FBI. Appalachian rivers usually have their whitewater running through gorges – rarely seen by roadside tourists. At Arden, however, the action was roadside – and there was more action than just the waterfall and rapids.

Arden Bar beckons right across the street from some of the finest rapids and local swimming holes. It's the kind of bar that sells beer in plastic cups because glass would just escalate the fighting. They also sell rolling papers, and if there were some more pot smoking going on inside, maybe there'd be fewer bodies flying across the pool table.

But the barroom brawls and drunkards in the swimming holes just added to the local charm. That and the tree branches that came crashing down across the gravel-paved road with every storm. No public works here – locals carried chainsaws in their pickups and created instant firewood, clearing road access within minutes of any such occurrence.

I had developed a fondness for the town and its riverside graffiti over the years. Just upstream from the Arden Bar one can view Moat's Falls, a 14 foot drop just above the place where locals swam and fished.

The river upstream of the falls provided a fun challenge for our group. Ed had decided not to paddle that day, as the Arden section was at the upper limits of what he felt comfortable paddling in his canoe. So he stuck with us and followed our progress down the river in his car, joining us when we'd scout rapids like Undercut and Classic from the riverbank.

Ed also stood safety for us, by positioning himself below the rapids holding a throw rope in case any of us got into trouble. Pete surfed joyfully on random waves, and Dick's river memory guided us through a technical section with multiple routes so that we could paddle underneath a naturally eroded rock bridge.

When we reached Moat's, the waterfall was little more than a trickle over rocks into a deep pool below. We looked at various options and chose to split. Dick and Wes opted to walk around and put in below the rapid beneath the falls. Pete and I chose to seal launch over the rocky lip of the falls into the plunge pool and rapids below.

"Here, take the rope," Ed told Wes. He handed off his throw bag as Wes began the portage. "You never know when you might need a rope. I've got another in my car." Meanwhile, still above the drop, Pete and I surveyed our options for running the rapids immediately below the falls.

"Well, we could run the center line over the rock jumble, though it is pretty low right now," I suggested. I never minded sliding over wet rocks, in fact I liked it, but most didn't and the water levels seemed very low for this line.

"Or we could just ferry across to that stream of current on river right," Pete countered. I looked at the options and saw a low-lying shoal of rocks that guarded the entrance to the right channel. To successfully clean that line would mean pointing

107

upstream to ferry across a strong eddy fence, a raised mound of water created by opposing currents that could rebuff a paddler, and then swinging downstream into the channel.

I assessed the risks as negligible – missing the ferry would mean a flip on the low-lying rock shoal, nothing too extreme, it seemed. But I had forgotten a warning posted on rbp by Strok-4-Brok, an Arden local, about the dangers of that shoal in low water. He described how one of his neighbors broached on that shoal more than 15 years earlier and had to break the rim of his fiberglass kayak to escape because a submerged log had pinned him in place.

Evidently, that log had played havoc with other paddlers too, but only at low summertime levels, because with just a few more inches of water, the whole obstacle disappears. People had talked about going in there in a drought year and getting the log out, but figured that any river feature that could hold a log for 15 years could probably hold a boat and body pretty tightly too. Pulling it out could create a suction that would hold a body permanently. But I didn't recall the online warning, and so dropped over the falls and ran the channel nonchalantly.

"I'll go first," I said to Pete as we hovered in the pool below the falls. I whisked my way into the ferry, but the elevated eddy fence formed by the churning wave train hurling downstream rejected my efforts. I spun prematurely on the squirrelly eddy line waters, and came to a thundering halt directly on the rocky shoal.

"Oh, shit!" flashed into my brain. I knew I had to pull the sprayskirt and instantly jump out onto the shoal itself, the kind of quick-twitch action at which I sucked. In that half-instant of thought, my boat flipped, sank, and lodged deeply in place. I abandoned my thought of exiting; I had read enough kayaking accident reports to know that pulling the skirt now could result in broken legs trapped inside the boat.

I relied instead on my kayak paddle, bracing it firmly on the river bottom. I twisted my spine into an arch, which let me get my face level with the current. Without that paddle brace, I could not keep my head above water.

"Heads up! Keep breathing!" I encouraged myself as I struggled to hold my head and bodyweight up and around my overturned boat. Further contorting, I could see Dick paddling down below the chute, casually setting up to grab me as I came swimming down through. He seemed unconcerned, and clearly did not understand how tightly I was pinned, and that pulling the skirt would be a last ditch resort.

"Help! Help! Help!" I yelled over and over again. I could not see my other companions and wanted them to recognize my distress. I felt foolish and could not understand why I could not shimmy off of that damn rock shoal.

In frustration, I let go of my paddle and determined to use my hands to push myself off and around that rock. No luck. Well, no luck in pushing off, but big luck in finding my paddle still intact where I had left it. Had I lost the paddle now, I would not have the bottom brace option and would be forced to pull my skirt.

Always remember Rule #1 – Do Not Die. Chip Mefford wrote an essay on rbp about how all other river rules were subordinate to the big #1. I didn't know what else to do; so paralyzed in fear, I just kept wailing "Help! Help! Help!" like a banshee.

I knew Pete was upstream and my best chance for help would come from him. I could still catch sight of Dick paddling back and forth below the chute, now poised and ready if only my flotsam and jetsam would come straggling downstream.

All of us had taken Swiftwater rescue courses, and Dick was now patrolling in safety formation. I had no way of knowing that Ed, onshore, had already tried to reach me with a rope but it had fallen short, or that Wes was making his way upstream toward me. I knew they would be in action, but could anyone reach me in the middle of this large river?

"I can't believe this is how it's all going to end," I thought more than once, already seeing the write-up on Monday's Internet posting. I was tiring rapidly, expending all my energy on keeping my head above water as the upside-down boat sank lower and lower with every surge of current. Very soon, I knew, I would have to make the choice to pull my sprayskirt, and I was scared.

Today, for the first time in all my misadventures, I felt the specter of that stranger who kindly stopped for Carla. A pro-kayaker, Joey Beck, had drowned for eight minutes and told me that dying had been euphoric. I had experienced getting sucked down into such a deep, quiet place on the Gauley. Down at the base of Pillow Rock, I felt that sense of deep peace. *But I can't breathe down here.* I had remembered the need for air almost as an afterthought, and pushed myself away from the boulder into the underwater swirls of current that would jet me far downstream and back to the surface.

Gently, I dropped the paddle and let myself go, giving in to the siren song of a long, deep rest. My head dipped under the water, and I bobbed at the surface in my boat, tossed this way and that by the currents.

I thought drowning was supposed to be peaceful. This is not peaceful! I came to my senses and pulled myself back up. I had already expended a lifetime's worth of adrenaline struggling to keep my head above water, but I pulled some strength from deep inside and grabbed once more onto my paddle, which I had smashed into the river bottom.

I thought again of my baby sister Linda, and how she too needed more oxygen than she could get. I loved her more than anyone in this world. If my underwater exploration had felt peaceful, I would have stayed under and let myself go. It would be easier to die before she did. I thought about Donna and Barbara, my other sisters, mothers of my three nieces and my godson, and was glad that I had visited all of them recently. The children would have recent memories of their Aunt Kaki.

Now, I moved into a survival delirium. Every unnecessary thought and action shut down, the entirety of my being fixated

111

on survival. About two minutes had elapsed, and eternity was collapsing down upon me.

"Rope!" I heard the familiar cry that river rescuers use when launching a coil. I saw and grasped the line. Across the river, a blue-helmeted Martian-like creature wearing a funny outfit stood on a rock.

I no longer knew my paddling companions by name, though I had known Wes and his blue helmet for years. Somehow, I thought Ed was across the river from me – though Wes was lean and Ed had a belly – moreover, Ed never wore a helmet. Later, I found out that it was Ed who yelled "Rope!" loudly enough for me to hear it. I've heard that hearing is the last sense to desert a dying person, and for me that was true. I no longer recognized by sight, only by sound.

Hanging onto the rope sent to me by the blue-helmeted Martian comforted me. I stopped yelling. Help had arrived. The rope Wes held helped manage some of the strain of keeping my head above water, but he could not dislodge me from that position, across the river and slightly downstream. My rescue would have to come from upstream, from Pete.

"Rope!" I heard the call again, coming from upstream. The toss fell short, and I knew that I couldn't hold onto two ropes, a paddle, and keep heads up too. It was all becoming too difficult. I was tired of the struggle.

"Not another fucking rope!" I yelled back. Pete understood my exasperation and took action. He abandoned the rope and jumped in his boat. Paddling towards the shoal, he leaped out

112

of the cockpit and yanked me upright as his own boat whooshed downstream.

He shoved me forward and dumped me upside down into the current. I felt bubbles on my face again, but this time I was moving and FREE – my hands gratefully reached for my spray skirt and pulled. I hung onto my boat as I was swept downstream, but my paddle remained solidly behind, wedged deeply between the log that had held me and the river bottom. Dick paddled up as I exited the chute and gave me a tow to the rocky shoreline. A fisherman stood by and offered assistance in getting me on shore.

"I was drowning. I was drowning." I gasped to the stranger as if in explanation for my bedraggled condition. But he already knew that.

"You're in shock," the fisherman told me, "you're eyes are glazed over. I heard you yelling. I hated watching, not being able to help. Get out of the water now. Here, take my hand."

Upstream, alone on the shoal in the middle of the river, Pete yanked my paddle free, and swam down the rapid after me. Even as I watched, I started to lose my memory of what happened on the river. I even thought briefly about getting back in the water and continuing on downriver, so quickly was the horror fading.

Instead, I consciously struggled to remember the details, going over and over the event with my companions, trying to solidify the sequence of events in my mind.

"Let's go out to dinner, I'll treat." Ed knew a place nearby, and it was good but cheap. I wanted to buy everyone lobster, but we had turkey dinners and apple pie a la mode instead.

"Pete, I'm sorry you lost your Salamander throw bag. I'll buy you a new one." Silently, I worried about the rope hanging on a rock and snagging a swimmer, but nothing could be done. He had abandoned the rope in order to save me.

I felt such gratitude towards these friends, and such guilt for not being able to extricate myself.

"You did exactly the right thing," Ed affirmed. "Staying in your boat was the right thing. You never know what happens once you pull the skirt; maybe you would have been trapped." I still felt guilty, and somewhat stupid too. How ridiculous I must have sounded, yelping for help.

"You know," Ed continued. "I was worried about you when you went under."

"I did it on purpose, Ed. I thought I could just surrender and let myself go."

"I know. I could see that." We sat in silence. How could Ed "see" my feeling? By what sense could he perceive my intention? I knew about another near drowning Ed had witnessed, and that person validated Ed's sixth sense too. The world held many mysteries, and the best ones couldn't be talked about at all.

It's weird, you know, how the mind just wants to forget, but I struggled to keep the memory just as I had struggled to keep my head above water. And then my mind slipped back to Pennsylvania, where my sister struggled daily for her breath. Without a choice, without hope of rescue, Linda continued to struggle.

RIVERRUN

Part II: Chrysalis

Streams of Consciousness – Virginia
TMI Day One – November 3, 2001

When I heard Carol's voice on my answering machine, I knew my cousin, the Wall Street executive, felt suicidal though we had not communicated in years. Carol and I had once been close, and I missed her friendship. The chasm created by her ticker tape life amplified the sad and desperate notes in her voice. I called her back as soon as I got the message.

"I've been thinking about contacting a medium," she told me. Carol had lost her mom just months ago, and she got to the hospital too late to say goodbye to her while she was still conscious. "I swear," she told me, "even though she was in a coma, I'm sure she could hear me. She didn't die until I told her that I would take care of John." Carol's brother, the only male of his generation, didn't hold a steady job. My heart gladdened at reconnecting with my cousin after all these years.

"Carol, I know she heard you." And I proceeded to tell her about my own communications with Scott and my Dad in Mexico. "And there's more, Carol. Real validations. Scott was famous for hand-paddling hard rivers. After I told Lightning the story of how he paddled with me on the Barranca, she asked him to hand-paddle with her on Bloomington. She did it, and never even flipped. Not once."

"You told someone else about this?" I told her, yes, of course. Though the truth was, it took me months to get up the courage, and at first, only in private emails to people who I thought might be open to a broader view of reality.

"I get help all the time, helping me do my trades, but I never talk about it with anyone. Well, other than with Uncle, when he was alive." Carol and her family always referred to Uncle Johnny simply as Uncle. He told her that "the others" or non-physical friends helped him get a general discharge after he went AWOL from the Navy during World War II.

"Hey, that reminds me, I got help too. From Dad, in January, the day after Bush got inaugurated. He came to me in a dream at 4 a.m. and told me to sell everything, so I did. I felt stupid at the time, getting rid of all the stock funds in my 401K; now I'm looking like a freaking genius." The dot-com tumble in late 2000 affected broader markets in 2001, and I had made a single digit return while anyone who stayed in equities lost double-digits.

"Anyhow, I have an idea. Maybe something better than a medium. Have you ever heard of the Monroe Institute?" Carol said no.

"Yeah, well neither did I. I'll send you a link to their website, Carol. We could go there a take a course and learn how to do this stuff ourselves."

Truth is, I couldn't have cared less about attending the Monroe Institute's experiential classes. When Christie, Dan Dunlap's old college sweetheart, the one who inquired about his death in Ecuador, had sent me the link, I checked it out but didn't see the point of enrolling. After all, weren't the dead coming to talk with me unbidden? But Carol needed to communicate with her parents, and I wanted to reconnect with her, so I suggested we enroll in the residency program together.

"She'll never go with you," her sister Esther warned. "Carol does this all the time. We planned a vacation together in Aruba, but she never showed up. She's too busy with Wall Street to have time for us – but at least she paid for our trip."

I double, triple and quadruple checked with Carol, all summer long – even telling her what Esther said. She maintained her interest in attending, so I suggested a date.

"How about going in October when the fall colors are at their peak?"

"Let's make it November. I think I might be busy with some clients in October. I can't tell anyone at work; you know – it's like if you're Joan of Arc, don't tell anyone you hear voices or they'll burn you at the stake." So we each scheduled and paid for the "Gateway Voyage," the Monroe Institute's introductory residency program for the first week in November 2001.

On September 11th, I watched the second plane crash on TV, and remained glued to the television for the next 48 hours, flipping through the channels, unable to avert my eyes to the tragedy unfolding. Carol watched the towers crumble in person, on the streets of the financial district, and knew many of the victims.

I canceled my plans to attend Gauley Fest that year.

"C'mon, Mothra," Julie chided. "No one's going to blow up a bunch of boaters in West Virginia." But the reticence I felt about the river had quadrupled since 9/11, and the post-trauma for me was particularly severe. During the blackout period when no commercial jets flew, the sounds of the military air traffic over my home on Lake Linganore, just miles from Camp David, sent my heart racing. I'd forgive Carol for backing out now.

"I'm definitely going," she told me in Pennsylvania. I drove up to visit my sister Linda when I backed out of going to the Gauley, and Carol decided to visit too. "I'm so impressed by all the research they've done. TMI is a very credible organization."

I checked back with her in late October, one more time, a week before our Gateway program started.

"Hey, Carol, are you driving down to Virginia or flying? I can pick you up at airport if you like, or you can come here and we can drive down together."

I won't repeat the string of profanities and rage that came out of me when she said she wouldn't attend after all. But trust me, I was brutal.

Someone from the institute called me the next day. "We know you're to room together, and we've been trying to contact your cousin. She never made her final payment, and we weren't sure if she was coming. I mean, looking at her address, we thought that maybe. . . ." My rage swelled up again, when I realized that she hadn't even canceled her spot with TMI, leaving the registrar wondering if maybe she had been a victim too.

"No, she's alive, just absolutely self-absorbed and inconsiderate. If you've got a waiting list, please offer her spot to someone else. She won't be attending." My blood pressure zoomed, and I thought of how I just wasted $1600 on a vacation I didn't really want to take.

My rage settled into a crick in my neck, which tormented me during the four-hour drive to the institute. I felt hurt, angry, betrayed. Maybe Carol had so much money that she could cancel vacations on a whim, but since I had paid, I was going. Besides, I loved the Blue Ridge Mountains.

As I drove down through the Virginia countryside, I remembered how I had discovered Skyline Drive after my Dad died. For some reason, the gentle ridges of the Appalachian skyline offered solace no human energy could provide. I returned there to grieve again, after Victor and I had separated, and returned home with a battered livery canoe. It wouldn't be so bad, this vacation.

I had no idea at the time that Bob Monroe, a former radio producer and media executive, had plowed his self-made millions into the research and education organization bearing his name. Monroe had a series of spontaneous out-of-body experiences (OBE) starting in 1958 when he was 43 years old, the kind where he looked down from the ceiling at his body, and thought he must either be going crazy or dying.

He convinced Charles Tart, a psychology grad student, to hook him up to the equipment in the University of Virginia's sleep lab, so as to see what was happening to his brain during his episodes. Distinctly different brain wave patterns did emerge during the sessions – and Monroe began investigating audio technologies using frequency following response and later binaural beats, so as to learn how to control his own experiences, and also to see if the out-of-body experience could be replicated in others.

Monroe patented his technology as Hemi-Sync®, and developed different frequency patterns to foster expanded states of awareness he called Focus Levels. He had started this research with friends in the Virginia countryside, but after the publication of *Journeys Out of the Body* in 1977, he attracted a myriad of famous physicians, scientists, and even emissaries from government agencies who were interested in his goings on.

Meanwhile, Tart became an internationally recognized professor and parapsychologist, and helped Monroe get that first book published. Tart retains a seat of the Monroe Institute Board of Advisors, but Monroe died in 1995 shortly after the completion of his third book.

Driving through Virginia with a migraine and a stiff neck, I knew none of this. I only knew that I had paid for a vacation I never would have attended on my own, but determined to make the best of it anyway. Besides, I kayaked sporadically now, having gotten spooked – so many river deaths and my own near

124

drowning. Most of my river time that summer was teaching Swiftwater rescue classes for a local club.

It was November again, and maybe nothing bad would happen this year. I hadn't thought of that back when Carol suggested the dates. Who knows? Maybe some of her non-physical friends, the ones who told her how to play the market, told her to steer clear of me in November.

I breathed deep the mountain air as I passed over Afton Mountain, said to be the basis for the locale of *The Waltons,* one of my Dad's favorite TV shows. I loved being back in the Blue Ridge, my personal place of renewal. And a little meditation could be good for me. I did know that they used some special recordings here, laced with the Hemi-Sync, to facilitate that.

As I entered the back roads of Nelson County, I let better feelings float through me like falling leaves, ignoring the persistent ache in my neck. This part of rural Virginia lacked the stately elegance of Albemarle County, home to celebrities of various types who sought a quiet lifestyle, but it had its share of grand estates mixed in with country homesteads, handed down through generations. Virginia, birthplace of presidents, home of the Confederacy, housed some pretty funky secrets.

I followed the directions on the yellow sheet of paper, twisting uphill on deserted roads. I finally saw the gatehouse with the sign announcing The Monroe Institute. It looked small but respectable enough, but my instructions were to proceed to the dormitory building where our Gateway Voyage would be held. I made a right turn and headed up Roberts Mountain, following signs to the Nancy Penn Center, the building with a distinctive glass tower featured prominently on all of TMI's publications.

"After you put your bags in your room, come see me over on the landing and we'll talk a bit about your background and interests for the week ahead." Lee Stone greeted me. He looked a lot like the hooded magician painting on his business card, except the he had a sandy beard and oversized glasses giving the Monroe Institute facilitator an owlish look. I made my way to Room 5, which was unoccupied, and dropped my bags, quickly returning to Lee who waited on the landing.

"I like your business card," I told him.

"Thanks. I'm an artist, too. That's in addition to working here and my private practice in hypnotherapy and neurolinguistic programming in North Carolina where I live." I nodded as if I knew what that meant. "Karen Malik, your other trainer, has been facilitating workshops here for more than 20 years and still has a practice in transpersonal psychology back in California. You'll also meet Paul Rademacher, who will complete his residential training program by assisting with your class. He lives in North Carolina too, and used to be a minister. So what brings you here?"

I launched into my story of dead kayakers coming to visit me, and the unusual circumstances of my signing up. "Truth is, I don't know much about this place or Bob Monroe."

126

I guess that sounded like an invitation because Lee then launched into a spiel about which books I should read and in what order. "Start with *Far Journeys*. That's got the meat of what's happening in it." Lee walked me to the library and pulled some books from the shelf. "*Ultimate Journey*, is fantastic, but it only makes sense if you read *Far Journeys*, so if you can only read one book, start with that."

I nodded my head thinking – no way am I reading these books. What's so special about Robert Monroe? I'm just here on holiday to enjoy the Blue Ridge, and if I go floating out of my body that's cool too.

I remembered a woman on Phil Donohue years ago talking about astral projection, and I never doubted such things could be true. Kind of funny when you think about it, because at the time, I professed that when you died, you died. Or so I said; I certainly rejected traditional religious beliefs. Perhaps if people had talked about the survival of consciousness, rather than heaven, I could have accepted such ideas too.

Lee showed me to the Fox's Den, or lounge area, where Julian, a handsome young Brazilian, held court with Jeffrey, an older psychiatrist from Bellevue. I added my blonde to the afro-curls and silver hair around the table, as Julian launched into stories of how he learned to go out of body from a guy he met online. Though they had never met in person, there was much astral travel between Ohio and Brazil.

Before long, an angular woman dressed in black sauntered in to the room, introduced herself as Elizabeth, and looked at me pointedly. "So how long have you been doing energy work?" she asked. I was dumbstruck by the question. Maybe the crystal hanging around her neck mesmerized me.

"Huh?" I grunted while staring at the crystal. "I don't do energy work," I replied shaking my head. What on earth was she talking about? She seemed to snort, as if in disbelief. Her roommate, a thicker woman with long brown hair, lumbered in a few minutes later.

"Mars Datura," she said by way of introduction. "Sorry, but I have to sit on the couch, and stretch out my knee. I fractured it not too long ago." Mars had a comfortable look about her, in direct counterpoint to Elizabeth.

"Is that your real name?" I couldn't keep myself from asking. "After the planet, and the hallucinogenic plant?" I hadn't read Robert Monroe's books, but I sure remembered Carlos Castaneda's.

"Why, yes, I created my name. I have an affinity for the planet, and the datura flower is beautiful." Mars rearranged her knee into a more comfortable position. Quite a group of characters, I thought, and excused myself to finish unpacking.

"Hi, I'm Kathryn." I introduced myself to the woman I now found in Room 5. She looked to be about my age, about 40 or so, with a pert nose and bobbed haircut.

"Mikel," she responded, pronouncing it Michael. "I've been dreaming about coming here for 20 years, when I first read Bob's books. How about you?" Another one! But this one looked every bit the part of the suburban air force officer's wife that she was. No crystals. An unusual name, but one acquired at birth. She radiated the warm essence of a genuine life, a mother with kids.

"Mikel, I'm afraid I don't know what I'm even doing here at all. I was just coming because my cousin wanted to, and then she decided not to come. What's with these beds? They look like Pullman berths or something." I pulled back the drapes on one of the berths and peered inside.

"Why, they're the famous Monroe Institute CHEC units; specially designed to keep out light and noise. I think they might even have copper shielding. Controlled Holistic Environmental Chambers – Bob liked acronyms."

After dinner, we got to do our first exercise in the CHEC units. I discovered that someone had decorated mine with little Day-Glo constellations. I also had a choice of lighting – red, blue, and yellow lights operated from a toggle switch, and there was a swinging reading lamp with an ordinary white light for journaling after the sessions. Headphones were stored on a little built-in shelf, and an on/off switch let our facilitators know we were in our CHEC units ready to listen to the tapes. I clicked on my ready switch and clicked off the lights, my unit now illuminated softly with the glow coming from the moon and stars pasted on the ceiling.

I shut my eyes cutting off the glow, and adjusted the volume on my headset. Electronic music came through the headphones as we waited. Lee's voice come through asking everyone to please check that their "ready light" had been turned on. As the stragglers checked in, Lee told us that we had been listening to "Metamusic" – new age music laced with Hemi-Sync frequencies to activate bilateral brain coherence.

I had studied the concepts of left-brain thinking and right-brain intuition in college. Ironically enough, I even had an honors certificate in a multi-disciplinary program in consciousness studies. I knew that the two hemispheres of the brain communicated through the connecting bridge of the corpus callosum, but I don't know that I ever *experienced* true hemispheric integration until the Monroe Institute sent me two cassette tapes to use at home in preparation for the Gateway Voyage.

I remembered lying in my bed overlooking the lake, and clicking on the tape in my Walkman. Bob Monroe's soothing voice came on explaining how he was putting a tone in one ear. I heard a strong, clear tone in my right ear. He then said he would put a similar but slightly different tone in the other ear. I then heard an equivalent strong, clear tone in my left ear. Then Bob said he'd put both tones at once. Instantly, I heard a third tone, but this one was wavered. Bob explained that the third tone, the wavering frequency, was created in the brain itself and was not on the tape. This binaural beat was the technology that got both sides of the brain working together in unison. Not only right to left, but also front to back, and top to bottom. Hemi-Sync got me using my whole brain, not just the proverbial ten percent.

Tonight's exercise was a deeper exploration of Focus 10, or the state of "Mind Awake/Body Asleep." I had enjoyed the progressive relaxation exercise at home, where Bob counted us slowly from one to ten, as he gave us instructions on relaxing various body parts. I found the exercise quite enjoyable, and I suspected it was the Hemi-Sync signals that kept me from getting antsy. I did feel a pleasant heaviness in my limbs, but didn't experience the "colors" that my cousin Carol reported. *Why didn't she come? She's the one who wanted this, not me.*

After we completed our first night's practice in the state of "Mind Awake/Body Asleep" exploration, I became increasingly agitated by the Hemi-Sync sleep signals being piped into the units. Not bothering to notice that I could have just turned the volume knob to off, I stormed out with my pillow and blanket to sleep in the back of my Durango.

"That's better," I thought though the cold crept up through the floor of the SUV without the foam camp pad I took along on kayak trips. "Plus, I can see real stars now." I snuggled down into the cold, breathing little clouds of warmth into the cocoon of my blanket and fell asleep.

RiverRun

Osama and Bud – Virginia
TMI Day Three – November 5, 2001

"**E**lizabeth, I can't stand another minute in those CHEC units! I came here thinking we were going to listen to some meditation tapes and roam the hills, not coop up in these bunkers all day and night."

"But wasn't it fun? You were really good at popping your REBAL." Elizabeth referred to the Resonant Energy Balloon, an energetic encasement for our non-physical bodies that we were taught to create on our first full day. I imagined my REBAL as the "luminous egg" that Don Juan talked about in Castaneda's stories. Elizabeth had been my partner when we practiced both shrinking our REBALs and then projecting them outward. We stood across from each other "feeling" the energetic space around each other, first pulling our energy in and then popping it back out.

"Yesterday just about drove me crazy, hopping back and forth to those cages like jackrabbits." We had done four or five sessions exploring Focus 10 with energy bar tools, creating living body maps, and also in free flow exploration.

"As you like it. You can resist all you want." Elizabeth retorted kindly.

"It's a beautiful fall day, and I'm going to get out in it. I like this world." The last remark was a bit of a dig, because

133

Elizabeth actively made the rounds with everyone in the class seeking to clear her karma and end her cycles of reincarnation.

"You know, I've been sleeping out here," I told her as I stepped into my Durango to skip the late morning exercise. "See how much room there is when the back seat is down?" I stopped pitching tents on my kayak trips once I got the SUV. Now it served as my security blanket here when everything else felt so strange.

"Really? But how do you know when to wake up?" The institute had taken all our watches and timing devices the first night.

"Oh, I can hear the bells they ring to wake you guys up." It was nice hearing those bells that first morning, and reassuring too.

"What bells? There are no bells. They change the sleep tape to something called *Cable Car Ride,* a little clang-clang, choo-choo to wake us up."

"They don't ring bells? Nice chiming bells? I heard them yesterday and this morning. By the time I get inside the center, everyone is getting up and showering." What did she mean? I loved listening to the bells every morning.

"You must be hearing the sounds of the universe. How cool is that!"

I liked thinking that the stars were creating the chimes for me, and went along with the idea of a musical universe.

"Well, anyhow, Elizabeth, I'm taking off."

"What? You're walking out? Leaving?"

"No, I've just got to take a drive or something. I'll be back in time for the debrief session. No one needs to know, really." I looked at her steadily. We had been told not to drive, since we were moving into altered states of consciousness, but I needed a break and some movement.

As I started up my Durango, I had time again. Actually, I must have had time all along to be getting up with the bells of the universe each morning. But I looked at the clock that illuminated with the engine anyway, and figured I'd drive for about 20 minutes and then turn back. I enjoyed listening to the synchrony of eight cylinders as I rolled out of the parking lot, turning right at the base of the hill for parts unknown.

Yes! I was in the Virginia countryside again – the rolling hills and softly contoured Appalachian mountains that hospitably welcomed inhabitation. I turned right again and headed uphill. Small farms, these, not the big estates in Charlottesville and Albemarle county – almost more like the hills of West Virginia, this side of the mountain housed country folk. The type of people who actually knew how to do things – build a barn, trap a weasel, farm a bit of hardscrabble. I smiled and let my body rock into the curves; driving in such a land was my meditation.

Nearing the turn-around point, I waved to a guy with oily long hair and a beard working on his truck and spun around in the driveway just past his. He watched me turn around, and looked at my Maryland license plate curiously. He waved too, and motioned as if he wanted to talk, so I pulled over and lowered the window.

"Maryland! Whatcha doin' round here?" queried the bearded man with longish black hair sporting signs of gray. There was absolutely no way I was going to tell this guy that I was staying at the Monroe Institute. I'm sure he knew of the place, and of the affluent community that grew up around it, where the streets had diamond shaped yellow road signs with flying saucers, comically warning of UFO crossings.

"Ah, I'm from Frederick County and I love to drive the back-roads of Virginia." As a kayaker, I'd learned that rural folk identified with counties; never say you're from Washington or Baltimore. At this point, a friend joined him. He also had the grizzled hillbilly look, but this time with a lighter complexion and sandy-reddish hair matching his yellowing teeth.

"Like some bud?" he asked, pointing to a bridge spanning a small creek. "We'll meet you down there." I drove down to the bridge, looking upstream, wondering if they planted along the creek. Time was running short, I thought, maybe this wasn't such a good idea. I didn't want to get back late. I was ready to bolt, when a pickup rounded the bend and stopped.

"Hey, ain't you scairt?" asked the sandy-haired feller with the bud. To tell the truth, I was beginning to question myself a little. I mean, these were guys with bad teeth, but I knew plenty like them who were genuinely good guys. And I knew how to

136

handle them too. I looked right at him, and then at his buddy driving the truck, and then back to sandy-haired Bud.

"Well, to tell you the truth, yer friend here looks a bit like Osama bin Laden." Score! This was November 2001. We all burst out in laughter. Osama thought he'd take a stab at me now.

"You et squirrel?" I broke out in a shit-eating grin. I knew how to answer this one too. *Thank you, Teresa*, I thought, remembering stories the River Retreat campground owner told me about handling the wild game her Wild Bill provided for their dinner.

"Squirrel – hell, no! All those little hairs get all over when I skin those varmints." Our conversation digressed into various scenarios of game cookin' and eatin' and I was going to run out of snappy replies; besides, I only had 15 minutes to get back to the institute in time for the debriefing.

I thanked Osama and Bud, and hopped back in my Durango spitting gravel as I flew back to the Nancy Penn Center with a buzz on. Sure enough, my timing was impeccable. I walked in and joined the others in the Rug Room where we sat on the floor and processed our experiences.

This time, Elizabeth and Mars, were quite excited.

"During the CHEC session, I had a memory of a past life in China. I was a mistress of a feudal lord, who disfigured my face when I displeased him, so that I had to live on the streets begging." About half of our class seemed to have pretty vivid experiences during the exercises. I was one of them, and

137

particularly liked Focus 12, the state of "expanded awareness" where I entered into states much like a waking dream, complete with sort of forgetting bits and pieces when I returned to C-1 or ordinary consciousness. I took Elizabeth's report as such without any great notice until Mars piped in that she had experienced that past life with her current roommate.

"And even before coming here, I already knew quite a bit about one of my past lives in China. I was a male, and vassal to a feudal lord with an insanely cruel son. That son mutilated one of his concubines, and I came upon that woman bleeding from having her nose severed, and took her home. She remained part of my household, but she never reclaimed the part of herself that had been broken by the cruel son." Not knowing anyone who had past life memories, I was suitably impressed with the level of detail Mars shared.

"Recalling this life is significant to me," Elizabeth continued, "because I've been struggling with being a woman in a society that puts such value and significance on physical looks. When I told Mars about the experience, I was blown away that she had been my protector. Thank you." Elizabeth gave a small nod of the head towards Mars.

"Interesting!" our lead facilitator Karen, the one who had helped Bob Monroe put together the very first experiential workshop at Esalen, as she later wrapped up the discussion. "You know, it's quite common during these Voyages that we discover connections with people in the class."

"Yes, but maybe it's just projecting and imagination," Steve, our grizzled Vietnam vet chimed in. "Something that we need, and so we create a story around it." *That's the logical explanation. You will never die on a river.*

"So what do you think about that?" Lee asked. TMI facilitators tended to ask questions rather than supply answers. *But it couldn't have come from me, I'd never say 'never' like he did.*

Steve rubbed his grey beard. "I dunno. I have a hard time with reincarnation. I think this is it. And I'm still trying to figure my own life out." *Me too. Could that be what he meant? Never in any lifetime?*

At the end of our session, Karen wrapped up by sharing a few clues, reinforcing that we could make up our own minds about what we believed. "That's why we've come together, to explore the possibilities. 'Go find out for yourself!' is what Bob always said. From a psychological perspective, we certainly know that the impact of a past life regression can have very real impact." Karen's quiet voice filled the room.

"So consider the possibilities of connecting with that part of you that is outside of time and space. Could it be that all those past and future lives are happening right now, when looked at from a non-linear perspective? Perhaps it is possible to take some action in this body, this lifetime, which then ripples out and affects the outcomes of all past and future lifetimes too."

"Karma," I thought, "now that's a whole new perspective on karma."

Castaneda Without the Drugs – Virginia
TMI Days Three and Four – November 5-6, 2001

I just don't know what I'm doing here. I like the mountains, and I'd really rather be outdoors." I told Karen about skipping the exercise and taking the drive, omitting the part about the friendly neighbors. She listened, and offered that if I wanted to leave, she would see what she could arrange. I talked about the option with a few friends after lunch.

"Why don't you stick around a little longer?" Jeffrey the psychiatrist from Bellevue suggested. "You seem to be getting a lot out of it." I had told a number of stories of more communications with the dead during our debriefing sessions. I imagined he fancied my stories almost as much as Julian's reports of astral travels. I knew Jeffrey hoped to experience non-ordinary states himself so that he could understand his patients better.

We were developing a proficiency in moving into altered states of consciousness. We followed a protocol in which we first visualized our worries and then put them into an imagined "energy conversion box" for the duration of the exercise. Then, we increased our physical energy flow by "resonant tuning," Monroe's description of vocalizing vowel sounds in a western version of "aum." I found that the vocalizing rattled out any residual mind chatter. After our vocalizations, we shifted our awareness to creating our non-physical REBAL, and then affirmed that we wanted to explore the consciousness that was more than our physical body, and counted our way to the focus

141

level. In these focus levels, we shifted our senses to receive information through any perception from a direct knowing to visual symbols or a kinesthetic sense.

Most of our group did not have traditional OBEs like Julian, but many shared conscious dreams which resonated deeply. During one report of a ceremony in which we all joined hands around Mount Shasta, I spontaneously "saw" a snow-capped mountain though I had never heard of the great volcano along the Oregon border of California before that morning.

That evening, I finally met someone with a big bold Type A personality, someone like myself. Joe McMoneagle had been known as Remote Viewer 001 during his years in the recently declassified Stargate, a CIA sponsored "psychic spy" program run out of the Stanford Research Institute. The Monroe Institute had ties to the program as well.

Joe walked into David Francis Hall, just as we finished a remote viewing exercise, our first exercise in which we moved into focus states without Hemi-Sync support, and then tried to identify blind targets based on latitude and longitude. We had some small successes, but no direct hits.

Joe's stocky here-and-now presence brought real world solidity to the research that had been done. Engaging and personally tough, probably from the years he spent in Army Intelligence, McMoneagle personally trained with Robert Monroe at government expense. The overall program had a statistically significant hit rate, and Joe was one of the most accurate viewers.

His most prominent success led to the recovery of kidnapped Brigadier General James Dozier – when he was able to provide specific detailed information about the location in Italy where the NATO chief was held.

After his first near death experience in Europe, Joe started acknowledging his psychic abilities publicly. "When I worked in intelligence, I called it gut instinct. The abilities were always there. We called it survival."

McMoneagle showed us a video of an appearance he made on a TV show. The program had selected four different target locations throughout Los Angeles and reporters and cameras were standing by at each. No one knew which envelope would be chosen as the target beforehand. The audience watched as the Los Angeles harbor was chosen from a sealed envelope. As the live cameras switched to the scene in the envelope's photograph, a large freighter pulled into that part of the harbor.

McMoneagle drew the scene complete with the ship, which had not been in the photograph, only on live camera. The TV announcers were stunned, and Joe told us his secret weapon after the video ended. "You don't think I was going to go on national TV without knowing the outcome, did you? *I traveled into the future* and knew the outcome before even entering the studio." I was hooked.

After his presentation McMoneagle joined us in the Fox's Den, where we munched on popcorn and raw veggies. I approached him obliquely with a question that had been nagging at me for a while – could the Tsangpo expedition on which Doug Gordon drowned have been a cover for an intelligence operation?

"Say, Joe, did you know an army intelligence officer named Wick Walker? Maybe from Vietnam?" Wick had been the catalyst for the ill-fated expedition to Tibet, contacting Tom McEwan late in 1997 to see if his old kayaking buddy might have an interest. He and Tom paddled together years ago when they did first descents on Great Falls of the Potomac in preparation for an expedition in Bhutan. Turns out Joe recognized the former army officer's name.

After reading *Courting the Diamond Sow*, Wick's memoir of the river trip in Tibet, I began to think that he assembled the paddling expedition as the cover for more covert activities. Tom had taken a tourist trip there in 1997, and shared slides from his private scouting excursions hiking along the river. He had to admonish me not to talk about the expedition planned for the following October because, he said, there were others who would like to claim the first descent.

Back in September of 1997 when Wick first whispered to Tom that an expedition to the Tsangpo could be possible, Tom had no idea where funding would come from. Other paddlers from Europe and the U.S. were already in Tibet, had been traveling for years to Tibet scouting the Himalayan river from various access points. Tom had made a single visit, and *National Geographic* funded the team.

"What do you think, Joe? The expedition's ground crew included a couple of Foreign Service Officers on vacation." I

CASTANEDA WITHOUT THE DRUGS

had lived around Washington long enough to know that State Department was often code for CIA.

Joe grinned. "Sounds like they were doing some mapping."

Made sense. Tom showed me the satellite images, which the government had declassified in the months before the expedition. A large Chinese military installation loomed along the lower segment of the river in the photos he showed me.

Joe's presentation opened me to the concept of time travel, the theme for our exercises the following day. We had already explored Focus levels relating to conscious dreaming or mind awake/body asleep in Focus 10, and expanded awareness in Focus 12. The numbers were arbitrary, and had been named by Bob Monroe for convenience. Today, we were to explore Focus 15, a place in which linear time doesn't exist. A walk after lunch had provided me with a target too.

"You might want to think about going back in time and having a different outcome from your near drowning," Mars flipped her butt-long hair over her shoulder as we walked about the institute's grounds following lunch. Mars's advice felt as grounded as her lumbering stride.

"The mind doesn't know the difference between real events and those we process as if they were real. It may help you overcome the ambivalence you've been feeling about kayaking." I had shared with Mars how all too often, I drove to a river and then drove home. It was as if a depression had befallen me. A feeling that death could wait around any bend in the river. Or maybe I focused on the river's perils, because I

145

didn't want to think about my sister Linda. Death hovered about her now, though I pretended otherwise. She had survived two years; in my heart, I knew she couldn't make two more.

"Worth a try, Mars. Worth a try." Walking about with Mars felt connecting – she was solid and gentle in her assessments. "You know, I went online today – I felt that there was another river death. And there was – another guy in Ecuador. Guess I'm getting psychic, eh?" I belted out laughing, inappropriately. Ever since my own accident, I did that a lot. Post-traumatic stress.

My time traveling took a mysterious twist, however. Twists upon twists as it were because Karen told us that we were to do this exercise without Hemi-Sync. "Training wheels – the frequencies are just training wheels. All of these states are normal, natural, and accessible. Prove it to yourself. Focus 15 without any Hemi-Sync support. We'll call you back when the exercise is over." I decided to do the entire exercise in my Durango, its openness preferable to me than the curtained CHEC units, and I trusted in my own ability to call myself back at the appropriate time.

I sauntered out and admired the rounded lines and shine of the jet-purple chassis. I rolled myself into the back seat with satisfaction as I pulled the door solidly shut behind me. This vehicle was home. I always felt safe behind the blackened windows. No one ever noticed me sleeping inside if I pulled over for a roadside nap. Always comfortable, and now my magic carpet ride into altered states.

I relaxed with the late afternoon sun and counted myself from 1 to 10, and moved from ordinary consciousness into the state where my mind was awake and my body comfortably asleep. Once adjusted in Focus 10, I silently counted from 10 to 12, and entered a state of heightened awareness – a state where I always saw brilliant greens and purples. After relaxing a bit in the perceptions of 12, I counted my way to 15, to the place where I could bend time, and felt myself rolling back into a waking dream.

My body unwound as if I were undulating into a current. I wasn't pinned between a rock and a hard place as I was on the Arden. I swirled at the bottom of Charlie's Hole, the place where Scott had drowned. I had been stripped out of my boat and now I spun through the water languidly, no longer in the churning froth that had sent me cartwheeling and violently slamming upside down and into the vortex that sucked me out of my cockpit with surprise. A rift of violent water above me yanked the paddle from my hand, and I dropped down a layer into a water ballet of flowing tai chi movements.

I was Scott now. And drowning was indeed peaceful down here away from the rush of water near the surface where I had yearned for a breath of air.

I was happy to move and sway in the water, no longer desiring breath, until I succumbed into a happy dream of sleep. *Spaghetti – it would have been nice to join everybody for one last bowl of spaghetti.*

147

I needed no bells or wake up to summon me back. My session was over. I hadn't freed myself from my own post-trauma, but I had moved closer to an understanding of the transition. I moved back into here and now reality, and stepped back onto solid ground. I walked back into the Nancy Penn Center just as the others were gathering in the central debriefing room.

"I was Scott," I shared. "I experienced his drowning."

"Maybe that's why you're here, without your cousin." My roommate Mikel, the quiet one, spoke with such wisdom. She was right. I never would have opened to such an experience if I could have found distraction with Carol.

"You mean like maybe she wasn't supposed to come?" The room fell absolutely silent, and I got it.

"Like maybe I was so resistant that the only way I could get myself here was by having Carol want to go?" I pictured a superhero Future-Kathy traveling back in time, colluding with Carol's higher self to get me here, and roared a big belly laugh. "So I guess my Dad was in on it too?" I added, and only half-jokingly.

"Your Daddy loves you so much," Mikel responded. "Of course, he's helping you." I was beginning to think that life might be like a Star Trek holodeck. How often did I want to tell those characters – hey, you programmed the experience.

I was mentally ready for the last exercise of the day.

"During our next exercise, you will open your energy conversion box and release an emanation of fear. Perhaps, it's something like the fear of public speaking, a very common fear for many of us." Not for me, I thought.

"You'll release the fear and let go of the emotion behind it, by bubbling it away. Bob's put together some great sound effects to help you do this. If for some reason no fear surfaces, then just bubble 'nothing' away. After you've bubbled away your fears, you'll be asked to recover the memory that created the initial fear – maybe you were laughed at when you spoke up in class, long ago. See the precipitating event now free from the emotion you had attached to it. You'll have several chances to bubble away your fears."

I already knew what I would choose to bubble away. They weren't fears exactly – I knew I had something important to do, and the Release & Recharge exercise would give me the opportunity. Into the box I went, and released my first attachments.

"Doug and Scott, off you go!" I smiled as I bubbled away the two boaters who disappeared in great rivers never to be seen again. "I'll remember you always."

"Ben and Chris, you got in over your heads, as I did too. I release you now." I thought fondly of Ben, father of four, just like my Dad. Just like me, could have been me, drowning on the swollen upper reaches of the Stoneycreek. And Chris, who I didn't know, who drowned in the eddy we shared together on the Lower Gauley.

149

"Dan and Garland, somehow I feel that you were ready to go. I hold you here no longer." Christie, the woman who had suggested the Monroe Institute to me, had shared much of Dan's personal history with me. And Garland's sister told me so flat out at his funeral. So I bubbled away the memory of the final two boaters who died on the river.

In the debrief session, I shared my simple lesson – the one that my higher-self conspired to get me here to learn. It sounded so simple in the telling.

"I discovered that I had been holding on to their memories as if to prove how much I loved them. But I can be free of that. I have a sister who is dying, and she's the important one now, while I still have time to share with her." Time may have been revealed to me as an illusion, just another malleable dimension, but it's what we've got here and now. The fleeting passage of time puts urgency on love.

The Music of the Spheres – Virginia
TMI Day Four – November 6, 2001

After I experienced the emotional clearing of all those river deaths, I climbed into the Durango and fell asleep that night to the chimes of bells, the same ones that woke me up every morning. The last leaves of fall scuffled across the parking lot gravel, an earthly counterpoint to the bells, and whether the sound came from my own mind or from the universe itself mattered not. As above, so below.

The Milky Way sparkled through the frost on my darkened windows, and the very cells of my body vibrated to the music of life. The pattern of both morning and evening bells would continue now throughout my stay.

Relaxing at last, I lighted gently onto thoughts of my sister Linda. Linda charged into my life, into all of our lives, like a bolt from the heavens. She was born a blue baby, because of a defect in her heart.

Born with a backwards heart, her aorta and pulmonary arteries in reverse position, she had been whisked to a children's hospital in Philadelphia, more than an hour away.

"They took my baby away! They took my baby away!" Mom gulped out between heaving sobs of grief.

With that phone call, my childhood ended at age ten. "Calm down, Mom. What are you talking about?" Little by little, I got the story out of her. Something serious was wrong

151

with my newborn sister, my Dad had traveled to Philly with her in the ambulance, and my Mom needed me to pack a bag so that she could join them.

So in fifth grade, I wound up writing all of my compositions about Linda and how she had a *Transposition of the Great Vessels*. My previous fixation on Niagara Falls as a writing theme was now sublimated to a greater love.

The reversal of Linda's major arteries meant that instead of pumping a complete circuit from heart to body to heart to lungs, her returning blood just continued to recirculate to her body, and her freshly oxygenated blood just pumped back to her lungs.

"All babies are born with a small hole between the chambers of the heart. That's what kept her alive until we got her here in Philly and the doctors enlarged that hole surgically." Dad explained. "They've got a whole team of doctors working with her here. In a few years, they'll have to do open heart surgery. They say she's got a 50-50 chance."

My love for Linda never wavered though my world turned upside down almost overnight. For the first time in my life, I was given chores – washing the dishes every night and scrubbing our three bathrooms every Saturday morning. My younger sisters got chores too. Barbara set the table, and Donna cleared and scraped the dishes, so I could accept loading and emptying the dishwasher, but cleaning all three bathrooms by myself felt so unfair. How I dragged out those hours feeling sorry for myself as a scullery maid. But even then, I resented only my parents, and the burdens they put on me as the eldest, never my baby sister.

Old enough to change diapers, I also took on some of her caretaking, in which I delighted. Linda's lips and fingers were blue, but her eyes were clear and bright. She bopped up and down in her playpen, dancing to the tunes of Herb Albert and the Tijuana Brass.

Dad danced with her in his arms, singing "Lara's Theme" from *Doctor Zhivago*, whenever she cried. The doctors warned us not to let her cry – it could strain her heart. Imagine the most spoiled child you can. That was Linda, and we loved her.

Linda became our miracle baby when she survived open-heart surgery as a toddler – surgery that rerouted her heart and turned her lips pink overnight. She was only the fourth survivor of that surgery at her hospital.

"I can run and jump and play!" she exclaimed when she got back home. As a teenager, she unselfconsciously donned a bikini, totally oblivious to the faded scar line slicing down the center of her chest. What a marvel, what a wonder! How I loved her.

We forgot that Linda was different, that Linda was special. Later we would say that she had 30 marvelous years – it was only the first three, and the last three, which were difficult.

It was now two Novembers since her diagnosis of primary pulmonary hypertension, and the outlook was as bleak as her start had been hopeful. It meant the pressures in her lungs were higher than her body's, and eventually her heart would not be able to oxygenate her blood anymore. Already her body carried a load as if she were climbing Everest.

"Am I going to die, Kathy?" she asked me in the hospital when she was first diagnosed.

"Baby, we're all going to die." A nurse sneered at me, talking with her as I did, so frankly. My sisters, one of whom was a nurse practitioner and the other a hospital administrator, agreed. But five whitewater deaths in 13 months succession hardened my emotions like stone.

Linda went on a brand new drug, prostacyclin. The FDA had approved the intravenous drug without full clinical trials when all the control patients, who were receiving a placebo instead of the drug, died during the six-month course of the initial study. Pulmonary hypertension had no cure.

"I always knew I would die young, just not this young." Linda was 32 years old. "You know, I did everything right. Always exercised, watched my diet. I thought I could make it to 50 or 55."

"Linnie, if I could, I'd trade places with you," I responded, echoing the words my Dad spoke to me when I suffered a childhood delirium caused by the measles. "You know, I had forgotten that there was anything wrong with you at all. You've been so healthy all these years."

One of her doctors leveled with me. Linda's case was unusual in that she had those 30 carefree years; she was one of the oldest surviving *transposition* patients – many had complications much earlier. Though her diagnosis was *primary*

154

pulmonary hypertension, there were some indications that the Mustard procedure, which had corrected her birth defect, could have been an underlying cause for the high pressures that were building up in her lungs.

During the open-heart surgery, her surgeon, who had done his residency with Dr. Mustard, created a baffle within her heart to redirect the blood flow. Mustard's procedure changed the function of the left ventricle, which normally pumps freshly oxygenated blood throughout the body, to pumping the venous blood into her lungs. This left ventricle pumps with six times the force of the right. Speculation abounded that her high lung pressures could have been in response to pounding they received over the years.

Pounding. My head literally pounded with these thoughts and memories, suppressed but lingering just under the surface of my busy life, waiting for a break in the action to pop up. My kayak frenzy seemed now to be a contorted picture of my chasing Death so that he could not stop for Linda.

I had stopped phoning and visiting Linda six months earlier. Oh, I still called occasionally, but truth was, I was distancing myself from the inevitable. I had done the same with my aunts and uncles, separating myself by avoiding contact during the last years of their lives.

When they found my Uncle Johnny unconscious in his home, I finally flew to Iowa for a visit. He had regained consciousness by the time I arrived and was pissed off at awakening in a hospital bed. He refused all treatment, and we spent hours together pretending that we were sitting side by side on a riverbank, fishing.

He didn't shush me out of the room, as he did with others, because I didn't ask him to continue on in a life he was prepared to leave.

"I'm looking forward to meeting the ancestors," he told me. He wanted me to stay on, too, until he crossed over, but I didn't know how long that might take. I wished he could exit this world somewhere other than a hospital room, but I didn't know how to make that happen. After an extended weekend, I told him that I would be going back to Maryland.

Guilt prevented me from breaking eye contact when I said goodbye for the last time. I locked my eyes on his bright blues as I walked backwards step by step. How could I be so selfish as to leave, when I knew he wanted me to stay?

Uncle Johnny understood my dilemma, and forgave me. Because I couldn't leave while looking into his eyes, he broke the connection between us by closing *his* eyes. Even though he wanted me to stay, he gave me permission to leave by that act. How selfish I was in leaving him to die alone.

Here I was, thirteen years later, in my Durango, having learned nothing. My sister was dying while I went kayaking. The music of the spheres caressed me as I burst into tears, crying for all my sins of omission.

River Red – Virginia
TMI Day Five – November 7, 2001

A s I allowed myself to feel my sadness and grief, the crick in my neck and the lingering headache disappeared. "Stuck energy," my roommate Mikel called it soon after I arrived. I might have rolled my eyes had she not been such a bundle of loving sweetness in the offering of her explanation. Maybe that's why I was always in motion, to keep from feeling stuck.

Although I had chosen to stay on in Gateway, I needed a break from the relentless schedule of exercises. Karen supported me in doing the program my own way, so when Lee announced a silent morning, I took to the road again. I could be silent while driving.

As I spun out of the gravel driveway this time, I headed for the Blue Ridge Parkway, a ribbon of highway spanning hundreds of miles along the ridge crest of the Appalachians through Virginia into North Carolina. I discovered this road and the hiking trails along it after my Dad's death in 1987.

I left in a reverie after our Gateway class watched *The Power of Ten*, a short film by Ray and Charles Eames, architects of molded plywood and the chair bearing their name. The film started with a couple picnicking in a park, and then the camera spanned out tenfold showing a large expanse of grass and a tiny blanket. Pulling back the camera again, the streets of Chicago became visible, and then Lake Michigan, the

Earth itself and we gradually journeyed into space looking at the Milky Way, and finally into blackness and a few stars.

Back to Chicago and the picnic, the Eameses now took us on the same journey but this time magnifying in 10 times. By the time the magnification had reached 10 times 10, the subatomic view looked remarkably like the view in deep space – the microcosm and macrocosm echoes of each other.

For the first time, I knew the Woodstock era truth deep inside myself as a revelation. We are both stardust and stars in the making. An inner silence comforted me, and I stopped at an overlook to make some notes.

As I pulled a pad of paper from the glove box, a couple of autumn leaves, which had been pressed between the pages, fell out. I scribbled in tears about a memory shared with my sister Donna's eldest daughter, who reminded me so much of Linda.

> *Reminding Us that Death is Here with Life*
>
> *I opened my notebook and the Leaf fell out. I had collected it with Bessie some weeks before – in remembrance of her first camping trip, along Skyline Drive. Its life force was sucked out, and was now a brittle, yet stable cast-off reminder of the flow of life.*
>
> *I like to follow that flow – down rivers, down highways, ever in contact with the roily earth, with all its sadness singing out in melodies that still chime out with joy.*
>
> *The bumps are part of the ride – generally managed and controlled – no, not*

controlled. Managed and understood and accepted. Sometimes a serene flow. Other times a crashing torrent.

I returned quietly and caught the eye of Joseph, who put his hands together as if praying and bowed gently in greeting. Joseph was young, in his twenties, with his dark eyes and skin. Wearing a multi-colored woven shirt today, he had a biblical look. I nodded and lowered my eyes in return. I wandered towards the labyrinth, and took a deep breath before stepping in. Though it seemed like a maze, I could not go wrong; the path twisted and turned, much like a river, but following the path required only trust and took me inexorably towards center.

"Now we are going to explore Focus 21 – the bridge between physical and non-physical realities. This first visit will be brief, and it's an opportunity you can use to explore non-physical consciousness. Perhaps some of you may want to set an intention to meet a loved one on the other side. 21 works well for that – it's a place where physical and non-physical vibrations can meet." Our facilitators were smiling big Cheshire grins as they admonished us to take a bathroom break before heading to our CHEC units.

I thought about my intention for the exercise. "No need to contact Dad or Scott or anybody like that," I smirked to myself. "I think I'll try to contact Amy." Amy "River Red" Johnson had died facing her breast cancer head on. She and I first met at Scott's Memorial Service. We had become friends and kayaked together after she quit her job at Arthur Andersen to go on the road for a year.

159

Amy's excitement gleamed when she showed me the modifications she had made to her pickup truck. The interior had a spare battery powering a small refrigerator, and a built-in bunk. A custom-welded kayak and bike rack straddled the cap, which had day-glow images painted by Amy's friends.

"I took a year's leave of absence," Amy told me. "But I know the truth. I'm never going back." She didn't either. When her yearlong adventure ended in Washington State, her breast cancer returned, metastasized throughout her body. But she remained open enough to fall in love once more during her final months, never letting her cancer deprive her of living life fully.

In my CHEC unit, I released my intention and floated through the colors of the various focus levels following Bob's guidance until I reached the bridge of focus level 21. I perceived the bridge area to be as occluded as a London fog, and I extended my consciousness into the murk, silently crying out: "Amy, Amy! River Red, River Red, Amy!" Too soon, Bob was calling us back down through the focus levels. As with any introductory exercise at TMI, the time spent in a new focus level was brief.

"One, One, awake and alert. Welcome back to C-1 consciousness. Please feel free to journal and go right to dinner. We'll debrief the session afterwards." I swung out of the bunk pulling off the headphones, disappointed that I had never found Amy.

Elizabeth, the energy worker with the crystal necklace, joined me as I plopped my dinner plate down at one of the empty tables. "You know," she said, "21 is the place where I go to meet the ascended masters." I visualized white haired wizards in flowing robes. "But not this time." She looked at me quizzically.

"This time, all I found was *you*." She looked a little miffed. "You were yelling something and jumping about waving your arms." I burst out laughing. Elizabeth's description certainly sounded the way I felt, helpless in a fog, casting about, looking for my friend.

"Oh, Elizabeth, that's amazing! I was signaling and looking for my friend Amy, but I never found her." As I explained, a sudden realization came to me. "Oh! Guess I should have listened more, huh?" She smiled back at me, not miffed at all.

"Pay attention. Like I said, I meet the masters in 21." I laughed back, imagining myself as a master.

In not meeting River Red, I found a wonderful validation. Elizabeth had seen me in her non-physical world, with exactly the vibration of intention I had put forth. It affected me deeply, as a mirror-reverse image of the time in Mexico when my Dad and Scott first visited me.

After supper, I had a chat with Mars. "So I tried to meet Amy, but couldn't find her. I can't imagine she got lost like Patrick." I referred to the Patrick tape we had listened to the previous night in the debrief room. We listened as one of the original Monroe Explorers went into a deep trance state and started channeling a teenage boy who had drowned in an explosion on a ship more than 200 years ago. He didn't know he was dead, and didn't even realize any time had passed. He just clung to a log in the ocean until Bob, manning the control panels, talked to Patrick and encouraged him to follow the light and join his mother, who waited for him.

"That happens lots of times when there's a sudden accident. That's why so many of us went to the World Trade Center a couple months ago. Hundreds of us traveled there in the non-physical, so as to help everyone bridge across to the light." Lee had talked about the Lifelines program after we heard the Patrick tape. It was a graduate level program, one we could take after Gateway to do this type of service work.

"I don't know, Mars," I said, "the whole concept of not knowing you're dead is too ghastly for me to contemplate. I can't have it in my world." Even so, I recognized that if I accepted the survival of consciousness, Patrick could be a fact too.

"I struggle a lot with what's real too," Mars responded. "But I've done too much of this helping work not to believe in it. It's my experience – just like your experience with your Dad and Scott led to a change in your beliefs. Can you be open to it?" I told her I could, but I told myself stubbornly that I wouldn't let it into my world. Not to my people. They all followed the light. Next trip out to 21, I just knew I'd find Amy.

Remembering the Holocaust – Virginia
TMI Day Six – November 8, 2001

J oseph wore his long black braids twisted. "When I achieve enlightenment, I'll shave my head," he quipped. "Until then, I'm not going to cut it." Joseph, with his shirt of many colors, showed up on my next journey to focus 21. I can still see him now, wearing his orange striped tunic of some indigenous origin, sitting in meditation surrounded by white light.

During this journey, I set my intention to connect non-physically with both Amy and any of the non-physical energies of my new companions at TMI. A little quieter now in my searching, I found Amy at the bridge. Her hair was just as fiery as when I knew her in life, and she cloaked herself in flowing white robes. It was as if I had entered a waking dream.

"I'm a greeter," she told me, not in words but in a flash of brightness, and I understood. Amy had passed through to the other side quickly, as she had done most of her transition work on this side when her cancer returned. In the months before she died, Amy protested the G-7 summit in Seattle, took a complementary approach to both the medical and holistic options that were open to her, and fell in love with Kevin with whom she traveled to Ireland in her final earthly journey. Now she worked on the other side, orienting those who were crossing over as to their non-physical life options.

"Amy, how wonderful." I spoke to her with non-verbal communication and then threw her an information packet about my sister Linda. Although I had not read Bob Monroe's books, my classmates told me that in the non-physical, Bob discovered that words were more cumbersome than what he called rotes, or packets of information. I imagined such packets as computer data files, and found such tricks easy to do in the conscious dream state of Focus 21.

"I'd love it if you'll show her around when she transitions." Linda had talked about a book she read about the Rainbow Bridge, a place on the other side where abused dogs went to heal after their transition. "I think she's interested in working at the Rainbow Bridge."

I wasn't in Kansas anymore either, and immersed myself fully in this Land of Oz. Having accomplished my mission by having met Amy and sharing with her about Linda, I thought to look about for some of my classmates. I perceived the face of Karen, our facilitator, in the clouds of my foggy Focus 21 world. She was checking in on all of us, seeing how we were doing and making sure we were all right.

Then I saw Joseph, meditating cross-legged and surrounded by light. He was deep in and unaware of my presence. At that moment, the voice of Bob Monroe began calling us back from 21. I shifted my attention for a moment to see if Joseph had heard him. He remained in deep trance. I wavered, wondering if I should respond to Bob or try to rouse Joseph, and the Light perceived me and told me to go back to ordinary C-1 consciousness. Joseph was protected wherever he was. "Remembering the Holocaust" popped into my head as I shifted my attention to the slower vibrating frequencies. I knew

164

this message as a comforting explanation for Joseph's deep state.

I looked around as my classmates slid their back-jack seat cushions across the pile carpeting and sat in preparation for our debriefing session. My neck turned as each entered the room, casting about for Joseph's physical presence. I don't think I heard a word of what my companions were sharing, as I kept looking for Joseph to show up. Finally, after about 10 or 15 minutes, I raised my hand.

"I saw Joseph in 21. He was surrounded by a white light and in a deep meditation. I heard "Remembering the Holocaust" and I'm concerned about him because he's not here." Paul Rademacher, the residential facilitator in training, jumped up to go find Joseph, and the rest of us continued on in session.

I talked with Joseph later, and he didn't remember the specifics of what he experienced, only the intensity. He chose to sit out the next exercise so as to deal with the emotional discomfort he was feeling but could not understand. I shared the information I was given, and he nodded his head slowly. "I'm still trying to integrate," was all he could tell me.

I pondered the communication that I received from the light. What was it? I perceived it as a non-physical consciousness separate from Joseph. I thought back to Joe McMoneagle's talk earlier in the week. On his first NDE (near death experience), the one that awakened his psychic potential, he saw the light at the end of the tunnel. But on his second

NDE, he got to the light and saw past it – and knew that the light was not the endpoint. He ended his talk with a strange statement.

"Next time, I'm not coming back. And when I cease to be, so will all of you." Poof! I felt like we were part of some magician's trick. Was all of what I called reality just a big magician's trick, down the rabbit hole into the holodeck? Joe explained a little more to me later.

"Well, I'm not sure I said it quite like that. What I meant is that you're in for a surprise when you're done with your physical life because each and every personality you ever knew is already there on the other side waiting on you."

"So I'm still here and there too? That it's all a matter of perspective?" This was a lot of new information to take in.

"I-Here and I-There is simultaneous," Mikel chimed in, joining the conversation. Joe nodded and continued his explanation.

"The sole reason for you and everyone you know being physical is to learn, and not just from your own personal physical collection device, but from everybody you interact with you in physical space/time. Do you understand?"

"Is this the concept that we're all connected?" I didn't tell Joe that I usually felt pretty darn isolated myself.

"I am as much a part of everyone around me, as I ever was myself." I looked at Joe, trying to fathom how we were part of each other. Mikel added a bit of scientific perspective.

"I met a physicist from NASA at a dinner party recently," she explained, "and he said that everything was either mass or photons of light. That even though we seem solid, the mass in our body is actually very small and that much of the communication that takes place between us has to do with sharing information through these light photons that pass back and forth between us. Fascinating concept."

"Sure is. Maybe that's why we say 'I am more than my physical body' in our affirmation. It would also explain everything from how we seem to be tuning into each other's fields during our sessions. Is that how it works, Joe?"

"I've gotten a glimpse of the truth, I suppose. At death, I return to the being of light that I actually am, a true image of the grand creator. In the non-physical, I return to the totality of self, which is greater than any single soul."

"That reminds me of Joseph Campbell saying that we are how the universe perceives itself."

"That's what my experience tells me. I am the summation of everyone I have ever known. Everything I do to another, I do unto myself."

"*Parzival*. Joseph Campbell's favorite story! That's exactly what Parzival had to learn before he could win the Grail. I guess all the old myths are true, even if they never really happened."

Parallel Universes – Virginia
TMI Day Six and Seven, November 8-9, 2001

"Y ou will remember your experiences," Bob's voice brought me back to consciousness during the free-flow 21 exercise. I had been floating out there far beyond the physical reality bridge. How could I remember the experiences? I could hardly capture them as they were happening.

Even in the moment, I only saw disjointed snapshots – putting on a motorcycle helmet, things like that. Nothing I could hold onto even as the experience unfolded. Yet I retained awareness throughout the exercise – not sleeping, not clicking out into an unconscious daze.

"You will remember your experiences. And tonight, you will dream about them and understand even more." I silently affirmed Bob's intention. I dreamed lucidly, often remembering several dreams in a night, which I had been told couldn't be done. I even recalled dreams from my preschool years.

"Tonight, I dream about my experience and remember more." I repeated Bob's affirmation to myself again, and the music of the universe, my special bells, chimed me to sleep just after midnight. I snuggled down and drifted easily into sleep in the chrysalis of my Durango.

Around 1:30, I awoke with a start with the memory of four simultaneous dreams. Simple dreams. One was bicycling with Doug Ammons. The other three were unrelated and equally simple everyday activities, certainly not symbolic or complex. Just me in different times and places with different people.

I understood immediately. In one 90-minute REM cycle, I had four simultaneous dreams! I have not had such an experience before or since, nor have I heard of any other individual who has experienced the same. I knew that the dreams were in response to my intention.

Now I understood what had been happening to me in the free flow 21 state. I had experienced parallel realities happening simultaneously. With neither words nor conception of such an experience, no wonder I had been confused.

I snuggled in the warmth of the blankets and peered out at the stars that sang me to sleep and woke me each morning. The cells of my body tingled with a *knowing* from the experience. Time really was as fluid and flexible as any dimension. The bigger part of me was outside of time, and I had just experienced an aspect of my total self.

A picture started growing for me, the seeds of which had been planted on reading Gary Zukav's *Seat of the Soul*. My sister Linda told me that this book helped her move past anger into acceptance.

I watched Zukav on Oprah. He said that we think of the Soul as being something inside of us, rather than us being just a fractionated part of the Soul. That made sense to me even then.

Now, I saw all my selves throughout space and time in a feedback loop of evolving consciousness.

Could it be as he said? Everyone is perfect, even our flaws being a perfect reflection of imperfection. And it was all so we could learn and grow in what he called the Earth School. We were here to experience emotion, so we could grow – and we were free to choose our lessons, in coming from either love or fear.

Funny, I had studied Modes in Consciousness in an honors program at Penn State 20 years earlier. I now felt like the kittens I had read about. How the kittens reared in a world of only vertical lines, did not even see a horizontal bar in front of them. They banged into it, because they couldn't perceive it, while the kittens reared with horizontal lines used it as a play toy.

Not quite at the level of perception of Joe McMoneagle, or Joseph Campbell, or even Joseph in my class, I still reeled at the insights I had gleaned during the past week.

Our class had taken a trip up to the Roberts Mountain Retreat where a Lifelines program ran simultaneously with our own. It couldn't have been the gain in altitude, this was the Appalachians not the Andes, but I felt stoned on arriving up there, and walked through Bob and Nancy's former home in an altered state.

When I walked out to the pool area, a couple people were playing drums, and when I quipped something about it being too cool to skinny-dip, the guy said something about

171

Esalen. Esalen – what was Esalen about? Vaguely, I remembered my Dad bringing some books home from the library. Naked people, encounter groups, something along those lines. It seemed important now.

I wondered how my life would evolve. Somehow, I had a sense that I had entered a labyrinth like the one I had walked earlier in the week. A labyrinth, not a maze, where all the twists and turns led inevitably to center, if only I would follow along. I had virtually danced the red clay labyrinth on the institute grounds, though I had entered it with some fear and trepidation, as if I could lose my way.

I knew that I would take Heartlines next, but had not yet made a commitment as to when. Mars had already signed up for two of TMI's graduate programs, Guidelines and Lifeline back to back in February, and asked about getting together in the brief interlude between classes. Ironic that I was thinking about taking another class at all considering how I had almost walked out.

On our final evening, we received certificates of completion, and I finally took a few notes. I didn't take notes at all during the week, maybe at first out of resistance and later in a kind of reverse snobbery, that I could remember my visions without putting pen to paper. But on that last evening, I made some notes. Notes about not judging myself, and letting go of anger.

Karen encouraged us to take a gentle reentry into the quotidian world, and I knew how I would do that. I drove slowly up the Blue Ridge parkway, and entered the Shenandoah National Park and Skyline Drive.

I pulled into an overlook in the southern section of the park, and joined a family – Mom, Dad, Sister, Brother. My senses were in slo-mo, as if I had been tripping on something other than sound waves for a week. Just an ordinary family, and all seemed so disjointed and unaware.

Except one.

The boy seemed to be about seven, and looked a little loopy wearing a bicycle helmet but no bicycle in sight. He looked right in my eyes, and I looked back and really saw him. We kept each other in sight, and his sister made a random comment.

His mother noticed and laughed and said that her son had an imaginary pet dog. I followed the boy's gaze, and though I couldn't see the dog, I could follow the energy and watched a trail disappear into the woods across the road. The boy looked at me and smiled, knowing I had seen it too.

I left the roadside feeling happy, and glad that I could validate one small child's vision. I took my time returning to Maryland.

RIVERRUN

The City of New Orleans – West Virginia
Tygart River Basin, February 2002

"There's this Russian fable about the seven-mile boots. When you put on these special red boots, each stride is seven-miles long. That's what's happening to you," Mars told me when we got together for the weekend a few months later. "You're developing very quickly. And it's going to be hard for you to understand why others can't follow along. That's where compassion comes in. It would be best to open your heart, so you can understand."

I shuffled along the creekside road that would lead us to Moat's Falls, the place where I almost drowned the previous summer. Mars walked briskly even with the slight limp she retained after fracturing her kneecap. I felt torn. Part of me liked the idea of seven-mile boots; I had, after all, moved into the wider levels of consciousness quite easily during the Gateway program. Another part of me just wanted to be normal, to be accepted. When we patterned for the future at the end of our Gateway program, I affirmed: "*I am full of light and love, and others are drawn to me.*"

I felt accepted around Mars, not like the freak I felt myself to be. I guess that's why I liked kayaking – it seemed to smooth out the rough edges in my personality, at least while I was on the water. Kayaking had been my only method of truly relaxing. "It's about being in the now," I told *Outdoorplay* when they interviewed *Mothra*, the outspoken denizen of the

Internet. "No past, no future, just a paddle stroke into the eternal now."

Once when I came back from a business trip, the airport parking service I used gave me a little card that tested moods. I would put my finger on the dot after I kayaked, and the mood-dot turned a cool blue. Any other time, I tested uptight black, or at best a stressed-out orange. My week at the Monroe Institute gave me a new tool to turn blue. I began to wonder if what I really craved was the sensation of being totally at peace, and I associated that sensation with the aftermath of a joyful day on the river.

"I've started practicing Tai Chi, Mars. I like it. Funny thing is, I tried it six months ago and got nauseous during my second class. I think it was because I was so profoundly relaxed, and it scared me. But I decided to have another go at it, and I'm hooked." I also noticed that my mood-dot turned blue after Tai Chi class.

Mars and I turned upstream when the tiny creek met the mighty Tygart River near Arden, West Virginia. I rented a creekside bungalow from Strok-4-brok, my paddling friend who had introduced me to many of his favorite runs here, the one that had posted the online warning about dangers of the log and the rock where I had gotten pinned. I called Strok, asking if I could rent his cabin for the weekend, when Mars suggested getting together this February weekend between her graduate classes at the Monroe Institute. I wanted to revisit the place of my trauma in a non-paddling situation.

"Want to see where I almost drowned?" I asked her as we rounded the corner and walked uphill towards Moat's Falls. I had a need to revisit the scene and I played it brave, but my butt involuntarily clenched in fear as we walked out in rocks along the shoreline and I pointed out the shoal with the hidden log.

"Last month, I came back here and you couldn't see the rock at all. The river was swollen brown and churning, and heaving with icebergs that had broken up on the flat stretch upstream." I didn't tell Mars that I had donned my dry suit to paddle Teter Creek, but the post-trauma had gotten to me, and I told my companions that I'd run shuttle for them instead. Where was *Mothra* now? Wouldn't I rather have her back? What good were seven-mile boots anyway?

But I couldn't bring myself to tell her the truth. Feeling scared, fear of failure still threatened my sense of identity. So I closed my eyes instead, and reveled in the memory of paddling, before I almost drowned. Strok and I had paddled Teter Creek about this time last year, and he broke two paddles getting down, so I lent him my spare, and then took his wooden paddle for repair at Jim Snyder's place on my drive home.

Next day, we kayaked the Middle Fork of the Tygart, a pristine jewel of crystal blue. I cleaned the large drops and led through the big boulder choke rapid, spurred on by beauty of the overhanging hemlock branches covered lightly in snow.

Losing my paddling persona hurt more than losing my marriage. So like a co-dependent lover, after I arranged to rent the cabin, I booked a scenic train ride along the Tygart Gorge. I had never run that particular stretch, and we got to clamber aboard a railcar from the historic City of New Orleans train, popularized by Arlo Guthrie in song.

I didn't tell Mars that I had never run the Gorge, and it saddened me to realize that I probably never would. Still, I recognized all the major rapids, calling out "Look, there's Shoulder Snapper!" as we passed them.

My losing heart towards whitewater, I finally realized, was inexorably related to Linda's downhill slide. For a time, I had sought to run away from the reality, plunging myself towards oblivion; not really wanting to die myself, but not wanting to face what I knew to be true – my baby sister was dying.

I could no longer deny the inevitable. Linda was hospitalized, struggling with pneumonia. I overcame my reluctance to visit her, and drove up to Pennsylvania the weekend before the weekend with Mars. My mind wandered back to the hospital visit.

Her slightly blue lips smiled when I arrived. She looked much frailer than she had at Christmas, with her shoulders curled forward, and IV tubes sprouting from the top of her pajamas.

"I'm so sorry, Linda. I wish I had visited you more when you were well. Not like this." Linda smiled wanly, and said it was OK. "I can't explain it, Linda. It's as if I think I can make you perfectly fine by not seeing you in person, though I know the truth. I did the same with Aunt Margie. And Uncle Johnny.

178

Can you forgive me?" Linda indicated that she understood, and pitched forward into a fit of coughing.

"You sound like me now." I referred to the chronic bronchitis, which laid me up for weeks at a time three or four times each year.

"You know, the articles I've been reading say that pulmonary hypertension is often secondary to scleroderma," Linda told me. Scleroderma was another one of those incurable diseases that seemed to run in my family – one for which I had signs and symptoms. Also known as systemic sclerosis, scleroderma attacked the connective tissue of the body, cross-linking collagen fibers into leather-like twists.

"Yeah, I know. Maybe I'll go first." God knows I wanted to go first. They say that dead people never tell you anything useful, but Dad sure helped me out with my retirement fund, telling me to sell as I did. That following May, while camping at the Cheat Fest, I had another dream, but one that I only half-held as a prophecy.

"Dad told me in a dream that I would die first, before you, Linda." I didn't tell her that I guessed I blew it by not drowning. "That's hopeful, isn't it?"

Coming back to the present, I asked Mars another question. "Why, Mars, why me? I'm not sure I want dead people visiting me, or seven-mile boots. Maybe I'd be happier with a white picket fence. This is all so difficult; I don't want it. Don't you see? Can't I just be normal?"

Mars started to answer then stopped for a moment, as if she was receiving information from her guides. She was not quite as dramatic as Elizabeth who cocked her head as if trying to listen more intently, but I was sure Mars was downloading information from some other source.

"Oh, yes. Hmmm. Yes, you don't want any of this in your present incarnation, of course. But there's an incarnation of you, two lifetimes out that needs your development right here and now. Hmmm. Yes. You're working with a group of individuals, paradigm shifters." I started with this revelation. Everything I did in this lifetime contributed to important work I was doing for the planet, two incarnations hence. I forgot my fantasies of a picket fence.

"Yes, you're working together to shift the paradigm of the planet. It's *that* you, two incarnations out, that's asking you to move forward in this lifetime. You see, it's all interlinked. The more you develop here, the more that individuation of you can move forward. You've got a lot of personal power – you move with your third chakra quite competently. You're a natural manifestor. Yes, that's what's happening. That's why you're being pulled forward with the seven-mile boots."

And crazy as it sounds, Mars's explanation made sense to me. Something inside of me turned, and I no longer questioned why. Being a paradigm shifter felt worthy, and I wanted to be worthy of such an honor. I would move forward into these realms, because it was important. I didn't know what Future-Kathy was doing, but I wanted in.

"Well, OK, Mars. I guess if that's the case, we need to visit the only paradigm shifter I know this weekend. He doesn't live far from here. His name is Jim Snyder, and he makes his living designing boats, making paddles, and he's even working on a custom jet plane."

Jim had been named a "Legend of Paddling" by *Paddler* magazine because he took kayaking cubic, shifting the paradigm of a two-dimensional sport, paddling on the surface of the water.

"He designs squirt boats, Mars, kayaks that are so thin they can slice underwater on eddy lines. On strong eddy lines, the boat disappears underwater. It's called a mystery move, and the kayaker spins and swirls down deep and finally pops up five or ten seconds later downstream. We're going to go visit Jim!" Squirt boating was an obscure but revered aspect of whitewater kayaking, and it shifted the paradigm from surface boating to the three dimensional freestyle play that came to dominate the sport.

Years later, Mars told me that she never forgot the look of steely determination in my eyes when she told me why I needed to move forward. Neither did I. Though I couldn't see my face, I remember how I felt because I felt a change inside me.

I knew time to be malleable from my final journey in 21, as revealed by my four simultaneous dreams. Besides, Linda was sliding downhill and I knew it. Our time together in this incarnation was running out. Maybe what little I had learned in this lifetime could be of use to her. Right here and now.

Linda's Choice – Pennsylvania
Children's Hospital, October 2002

e had learned a lot from my Dad's illness, my family and I. He had been increasingly tired and clumsy, and felt short of breath. When the doctors finally diagnosed him, we breathed a sigh of vindication; he was tired of being treated like a psych case. But this diagnosis of ALS, what could we expect? Dad said he remembered listening to Lou Gehrig on the radio when he retired from baseball. The prognosis was bleak – he would totally lose the use of his muscles, all his muscles – those that let him walk, those that let him eat, those that let him breathe.

When my sisters and I assembled in our childhood home for Mother's Day 1987, Dad told us that it might be the last time we assembled as a family. And he was right. By July, he chose his exit, preferring liberation of the spirit to having a mind trapped in a body, unable to communicate.

Thanks to a continuous IV pump infusion of expensive medication, Linda survived beautifully by continually adjusting to her limitations and challenges with a positive outlook towards what she still had, rather than what had been taken away.

"A pacemaker – no! – I'll look horrible in a bathing suit," had given way to the acceptance that she would never be able to swim again.

"See! Being disabled isn't so bad," she chuckled as she pocketed her free National Parks pass. "When I get worse, Kevin and I will get an RV and tour the country together. Do you want to come to Alaska with us?" By the time they bought the RV, however, Linda knew she could not stray more than a day's drive from the hospital. Still, she ventured out on weekend camping trips with her husband, always grateful for what she had, never looking back on what could have been.

As she lost mobility with more frequent hospitalizations, Linda developed an interest in bird watching, something she could do from her kitchen deck. During 2002, she found herself hospitalized multiple times due to infections. As the inevitable drew closer, doctors presented the idea of a heart-lung transplant.

"I no longer care about wearing my oxygen pump in public, or even about having to use a scooter in the grocery store," she told me as I wheeled her into a small brick courtyard that was part of the hospital complex in Philadelphia. "But if I go on the transplant list, they'll keep me imprisoned in the hospital. They won't even let you wheel me outside to see the pigeons because the protocols for getting organs are so strict."

A heart-lung transplant could cure Linda's condition, but accepting the option meant living in the hospital until a donor was found, the timeline being about an 18-month wait. Incredulous that being on a transplant list meant such cruelty as never leaving the hospital room, even to catch a bit of fresh air in the courtyard, I wondered if the doctors had been trying to put a negative slant on this option. I didn't want her to die waiting in a hospital room.

"They say if it works, it could cure me. I'd have a second chance at everything. But I don't know. I feel like I had my miracle when I was born." I could only imagine Linda's internal struggle. It had been tough enough for me to choose back surgery after the fall I had taken when swatting at a moth. And it wasn't until I was crawling across the living room floor on my elbows, that the decision for surgery was crystal clear.

"You were a miracle indeed – only the fourth baby with a successful outcome from the Mustard open heart surgery at Saint Christopher's Hospital. I think it was because you were so tough – spitting mashed potatoes at the nurses and all." We smiled at the memories of family lore. "Do you really remember back to that surgery? You were barely two years old."

"I remember waking up and they were counting something. Then someone noticed, and they put me back to sleep." The afternoon sun, now obscured by the tall center city buildings, fell into shadow, and with the change a chill came that sent us back inside.

"What did you think about Pnina's healing session?" I had hired a teacher from the Barbara Brennan School of Healing to work with Linda. I learned about the school while at a fancy hotel spa, and I sought help from it because visiting with Linda physically drained me. It almost seemed as if she needed my life force energy, and I freely shared it with her. But I thought there might be a better way.

"Oh my god, after she left, I fell right asleep. It was the best sleep I'd had in months." Pnina accidently left behind two small vials of essential oils – one with a pink label called Joy that smelled like flowers, and another with a green label called Valor with an earthier, more resonant vibration. "I wonder if we can keep the oils, I like them."

"Well, I've hired her to come visit you again next week. Looks like the vancomyacin is working, so you'll probably be home by then. I wonder why they fooled around with those other drugs for so long anyway." I had spent enough time in medical sales to know that she was on the antibiotic of last resort, and my intuition had told me that despite the promising lab reports, only vanc would clear the infection around her heart. I wheeled her down the corridor into her windowless room.

"Would you think I'm crazy if I said I didn't want the transplant? It doesn't seem like I should be turning down something that could cure me. Everyone seems so excited about the idea." Everyone except me, I thought. Double transplants were a big deal, and even if she could survive the surgery, were no guarantee of a healthy life.

I had a boating friend who went through a pancreas-liver double transplant. Nancy survived and it even cured her diabetes, but she had her challenges. Although the transplant was successful, she still went blind and needed a double leg

186

amputation because of all the nerve damage she had accumulated over the years.

"I wouldn't think you were crazy. Eighteen months is a long time to live like this – in a windowless room with no natural light or air." *Living here will kill you, Linda. Life is short, no matter how we number the years.*

"A nurse told me about an 18 year old boy who had a transposition and pulmonary hypertension, just like me. She said he died waiting, here in the hospital. That's my nightmare – to die alone in the hospital." *You can choose life over time, Linda.*

"I think that's why I'm afraid to go to sleep; I'm always afraid that I'm going to die, and that I'll be alone." *If you stay in the hospital, we'll tire of visiting. It's likely that could happen.*

"Here, let me rub your feet and chest with those oils. Try and get some rest. I'll be right here by your side." I opened up the green bottle, and the fragrance of the woods came forth as I speckled some drops on the soles of her feet.

"Breathe in the good air, and ask your higher self, the part of yourself that is outside of time, what to do. She already knows the outcomes. Ask that part of yourself for guidance." Linda started breathing more slowly and steadily. I opened up the pink bottle called Joy, and the smells of a garden burst forth.

"You know when you were little, we always dressed you in pink. We always wanted to brighten the blues of your nails and

187

lips." I rubbed the oil against the palms of my hands and held them over her nose and mouth. I then gently touched down on her chest moving aside the tubes carrying medication directly into her heart. "I love you, Pubba."

I sat with her some hours, and then the phone rang. "Hi Kevin, she's resting. Yeah, she's doing better." Linda sprang awake on hearing Kevin's name, and motioned me to give her the phone.

"Kevin," she whispered in a little girl voice. "I don't think I want a transplant. I think I want to come home."

Epilogue: Five Novembers

L inda went home that October, and spent the next five months living joyfully with her husband Kevin, and her two labs, Molson and Cinder. She died the following April, in full consciousness, with her husband holding her hand, her mother rubbing her feet, and her sisters surrounding her, singing. She opened her eyes one last time before crossing over, and as she did, a single tear dropped down her cheek.

Sylvia Browne, the psychic, says that we come into the world with five preprogrammed exit points. I certainly chose not to take my exit point on the Arden, despite my bravado in saying that I wanted to die first. Linda, the way I see it, was simply out of exit points.

She could have died at birth. And then there was the surgery on her lungs, which needed to be done before she could have the open-heart surgery as a child. Our bodies are such amazing equipment; hers sought to supplement oxygen to the lungs by creating new pathways, new arteries that needed to be cauterized before the corrective procedure on the heart. She could have exited then or during the open-heart surgery months later, two more exit points skipped. In first grade, she complained of "weak knees" and it turned out that she had developed tachycardia, with her heartbeat racing at more than 200 beats per minute, another exit point denied.

Karma. I felt that her birth and death were intertwined in karma. She shouldn't have survived at all, and the heroic

189

operation that corrected her heart destroyed her lungs. Perhaps she had come to the earth plane to change me for the better. After spending that day with Linda in October when she chose against the surgery, I got the courage to start living my own authentic life.

Linda had invited me to go on a road trip with her, when she and Kevin bought that camper. A road trip she never got to take. Had she known that I had always wanted to take such a trip? She had only been a toddler when I opened up the pages of *Life* magazine, and imagined myself on the odyssey across the country I saw depicted.

So when Linda went home after all those hospitalizations, I got the courage to take a month off and hit the road. "You know, my sister's been sick, and I'm feeling the need to take some time off. Things are usually slow in November, do you mind?" My director didn't need to know my plans. I was on the road!

Didn't take much planning. A two-inch piece of foam, flannel sheets and down comforter made up my bed. And enough room besides to house a Rubbermaid container, a small duffel for my clothes, and a small cooler for beverages and snacks.

I visited Mars in Denver on my way westward, and Bryce and Zion national parks. I stopped briefly to visit a paddling friend, Space Canoe, in Los Angeles and saw him perform as singer-songwriter Ric Taylor while I was in town. I successfully avoided all other cities.

I drove up the Pacific Coast Highway, taking more than four hours to get from Morro Bay to Esalen. I planned a week at Esalen, the place I remembered my Dad had always wanted to visit. In choosing my bliss, I chose for him too. After all, it was my coming into the world, which caused him to pass up the writing fellowship at Long Island University. He became an ad man instead.

I spent that November on the road, calling Linda often, making it her road trip too. Returning by way of Sedona, I was back in Pennsylvania by Thanksgiving, and burst into tears after my first visit with her, feeling her death so near.

"What do you mean?" my Mom asked me. "She's doing great; she just went to a craft fair, and decorated the house all by herself."

I returned at Christmas, bringing identical gifts for my sister – pure silver heart pendants strung on a gold chain by way of a hole in the heart. I got one for Julie too. And returned to Pennsylvania again and again.

The year after Linda died, I took a longer three-month road trip. And then, I kept returning to Esalen, again and again, until on a third road trip, I finally moved to California, settling down on the ocean in Pacific Grove, on the very street where Joseph Campbell lived during the Great Depression.

There must be something in the salt air there because I started writing poems, and then I took up this story, writing about the Five Novembers that changed the course of my life. November 1998 – Scott dies. November 1999 – Linda diagnosed. November 2000 – Dan dies, like Scott on the day I am to meet him. November 2001 – Gateway Voyage, The Monroe Institute; November 2002 – On the Road.

Taking to the highway, I found that sense of connection, the inner peace that had eluded me for so many years. I felt as one with my family. Kathy, source of Strength. Donna, the Heart of the family. Barbara, the Glass of Champagne. Linda, the Miracle. Mom the Survivor. Dad the Dreamer. The sense of connection broke through space and time, reaching back and liberating all my ancestors' dreams as I fulfilled mine.

She only whispers of death
Whispers so softly that
          no words are spoken

No words are needed
          I hear her whispers

And I want to shout
          "Let me toss your limbs
          to the buzzards"

You're dying!
And the secrets
of the world are revealed
by a bluebird near the window

You're dying!
And so our own
returns to the clouds
Ocean no more

I'll look for you in the sky

Made in the USA
San Bernardino, CA
13 August 2014